THE BORDER

THE BORDER
LIFE ON THE LINE

Text and photographs by Douglas Kent Hall

Abbeville Press · Publishers · New York

Copyright 1988 by Cross River Press, Ltd.
Published in the United States of America in 1988 by Abbeville Press, Inc.
All rights reserved under International and Pan-American Copyright
Conventions. No part of this book may be reproduced or utilized in
any form or by any means, electronic or mechanical, including
photocopying, recording, or by any information storage and retrieval
system, without permission in writing from the Publisher. Inquiries
should be addressed to Abbeville Press, Inc., 488 Madison Avenue,
New York, NY 10022
Printed and bound in Japan.

Library of Congress Cataloging-in-Publication Data
Hall, Douglas Kent.
   The border: life on the line/text and photographs by Douglas Kent Hall.
      p.   cm.
   ISBN 0-89659-685-0
   1. Mexican-American Border Region.   2. Hall, Douglas Kent.
   I. Title.   F787.H35 1988   979—de19

To Wayne Hall,
Larry Bell, John Bigelow,
and Ray Graham

Editor: Alan Axelrod
Designer: Renée Khatami
Production supervisor: Hope Koturo

Jacket front: *Reynaldo Martinez and*
Tino Palao, Muzquiz ranch
Jacket back: *Nogales, Sonora*
Title page: *Ojinaga, Chihuahua*
Copyright page: *Near Juárez*
Pages 8-9: *Big Bend country, Texas*
Pages 250-51: *Sonoita, Sonora*

CONTENTS

How can life on the border be other than reckless?
You are pulled by different ties of love and hate.
                              —GRAHAM GREENE

FRONTIERS

1n the hot white sun, they slipped through the fence and trotted toward an old Chevy pickup, their bodies seeming to float like strange fish through the shimmering mirage pools. There were at least fifteen of them, all fighting to get against the tailgate to see something in the bed of the truck.

"Watch them run back to the other side," said the agent.

Wheeling the green Border Patrol 4 x 4 toward them, he tromped on the accelerator. When they heard the truck's stiff suspension hammering over the washboard road, the Mexicans turned to look. There was a moment of confusion. A few of the younger ones did flee, racing around the front of the pickup and diving between the sagging strands of barbed wire, back into Mexico. They waited there, in the safety of their own country, and watched us pull up. Behind them, huddled against the hillside, was the dusty little *ejido* where they lived—without electricity, without running water. One small boy reached through the fence with a thorny mesquite stick and pulled his straw hat closer to the bottom strand of barbed wire. He grabbed it and scrambled back. The older ones, experienced and therefore more intrepid—but still cautious—stood their ground.

The agent set his hat straight and got out.

Desperate cries, as if from a child in pain, echoed from the back of the pickup.

"*Que pasa—*" asked the agent.

"*Es un cabrito,*" explained one of the Mexicans.

The young goat had its legs tied and was struggling to get free. Its hooves clattered against the steel bed. The farmer, an old Mexican-American, had brought it down to sell to the Mexicans from the *ejido*.

We climbed back into the 4 x 4.

"You could've taken them in, right?" I asked, testing.

Earlier that morning, I had watched while this agent and two others on the ground, plus another agent circling in a small Cessna at such slow

The Sonoran Desert

speeds that the strident rasp of the stall warning could be heard constantly over the radio, apprehended a group of wetbacks in the brush a few miles from Columbus, New Mexico. Then, less than an hour later, we'd picked up a number of others, including one half-crazed individual suffering from too much sun or a serious overload of drugs, who was trotting north on the open road, a bowl of tortillas in one hand and a New Testament in the other, his sneakers sending up dry puffs of dust. They had all been returned to the border, booked in the office behind the Port of Entry, and sent back into Mexico. And it was only the beginning of the day.

"Technically, yes," the agent admitted, starting the engine. "But this bunch'll go back themselves. Hell, half of them probably work right here on this farm."

It was a reaction I'd seen in other places, from other Border Patrol agents. It seemed they felt that under the circumstances these were almost "locals," almost citizens, almost impossible to stop.

"What about the goat? It's not legal to take that into Mexico, is it?"

"That's the Mexicans' problem—"

I crossed over into Mexico in 1957. It was my first border crossing, and still it remains the most impressive.

That was a trip born of youthful impulse. I was a student, restless, impressionable, and I had spent much of my spare time that fall devouring the works of D. H. Lawrence. In an imported British edition of his slender but passionately written *Mornings in Mexico*, I had encountered two statements that fired my imagination: "when all is said and done, Mexico has a faint, physical scent of her own, as each human being has. And this is a curious, inexplicable scent, in which there are resin and perspiration and sunburned earth and urine among other things." Then:

> Nowhere more than in Mexico does human life become isolated, external to its surroundings, and cut off tinily from the environment. Even as you come across the plain to a big city like Guadalajara, and see the twin towers of the cathedral peering around in loneliness like two lost birds side by side on a moor, lifting their white heads to look around in the wilderness, your heart gives a clutch, feeling the pathos, the isolated tininess of the human effort. As for building a church with one tower only, it is unthinkable. There must be two towers to keep each other company in this wilderness world.

It was this kind of excessive romantic imagery, so typical of Lawrence, that convinced me I had to see Mexico. I was fascinated by all that he said, caught up in the promise of magic, and tantalized by the strange, dark savagery Lawrence hinted at. I knew that I had to go at once.

The next night, in a hopped-up 1955 Ford, a friend and I sped out of Salt Lake City. Wide-eyed from too much truck-stop coffee, we saw the colors of the morning sun scintillating from the stark, painted mesas of the

Near Texas Highway 170, east of Redford

Canyonlands at Four Corners, where Utah touches Colorado, Arizona, and New Mexico. With only brief stops for food and fuel, we put hundreds of hard miles on the Ford and rolled into El Paso sometime late the following afternoon.

Crossing the bridge over the Rio Grande into Juárez, into Mexico ("Old Mexico," I had heard it called all my life), was like a leap into a dark and sinister dream. It brought back every story I had ever heard about Mexico. I had been warned about the food, about the water, about pickpockets and bandits, about whores and disease, about the terrible treachery of Mexicans in general.

My paranoia primed and running high, I found along the broken, potholed roads plenty to support all these fears. Small groups of *vaqueros* with carbines slung across their saddles watched us pass; a pair of black shoes stood in the middle of the road—empty; and a few yards farther a hulking Dina bus, stopped, its passengers clustered outside and staring silently at the still, lifeless body of a man they had just hit with enough force to lift him out of his shoes; farther on, bonfires burned in the middle of nowhere, with *paisanos* in huge straw hats huddled around them, looking into the flames or out into the empty dark. There, on the border, Mexico was already everything Lawrence had promised.

In the years that have followed, I've seen the border many times, as I crossed into Mexico or came out at various towns between Matamoros and Tijuana. As a part of my early warnings about Mexico, I had been told that border towns were inherently, categorically dirty and corrupt, no matter which side of the boundary they were on, but especially if they were on the Mexican side, and I was advised, only partly in jest, that the best way to see these places was through the closed window of a car traveling at high speed.

Like a lot of other people, I trusted that specious judgment and assumed that these towns huddled along the border did represent the worst of Mexico, that, indeed, they could be numbered among the worst of cities anywhere. But the more I saw of the border, the more time I spent there, the greater my fascination for it became. I stopped thinking of this region as I thought of the rest of Mexico. In my mind, it developed a unique personality and a national characteristic of its own, as though this were a narrow fledgling nation nearly two thousand miles in length, with an indefinite and elastic width that would—and did—accommodate almost anything.

That the border is not quite what it appears is, of course, an understatement. In its ambiguity lie the complexities that have made it a thorny problem. Even where it begins and ends, except as the abstract line on the map and the more physical line of the fence, is largely a matter of opinion. Some people, for whatever reason, say that it extends for twenty miles or so on either side of the map's line; certain trade laws—notably on the Mexican side—have been relaxed to accommodate just this area. Others say the border includes South Albuquerque, parts of Houston, Chicago, Miami, North Denver, East L.A., Oakland, the Mission District of San Francisco, and wherever else the illegal alien population has crept. Curiously, the places just named are approximately the same outpost boundaries that existed at the height of the Spanish expansion north from Mexico in the seventeenth and eighteenth centuries.

Except for certain incidental considerations such as fishing and oil rights, boundaries delineated by oceans are relatively simple and easy to maintain. Inland borders are something else. They have been created by men to divide nations where no natural boundary existed. Almost without exception, these borders are the product of greed, war, and compromise. For this reason they are usually arbitrary, often unrealistic, and create troubles between people who might otherwise be at peace with each other. This has always been true of the line that snakes across the North American continent to divide the United States and Mexico.

In a special sense, the borderland today remains pretty much what it always was: the scene of an ongoing economic conquest. History is full of accounts of the heartbreak and triumph of men who sought fortune on this frontier. The great northward push in the sixteenth century was spurred on by exaggerated promises of wealth even greater than the Spaniards had thus far seen. Mexico had hardly proved a disappointment. It yielded vast amounts of treasure, the first haul pilfered from the temples of the Indians and the second mined in great quantities from the mineral-rich mountains in the central plateau of Mexico. This booty was shipped back to Europe to swell the treasuries of Charles V and Philip II and in turn to help give Spain an enviable position as a world power. Cities grew up around the mines, drawing people out of the capital; in time they became important industrial and cultural centers, which have continued to thrive into modern times: Durango, Guanajuato, Monterrey, Saltillo, and Zacatecas, as well as outpost camps in Sonora, Coahuila, and Chihuahua.

Given the proof of former successes, it is no surprise that tales of even greater riches farther to the north would attract the interest of the Spaniards, who had already been so successful in their conquest of the

New World. These stories of new and vaster treasures were as fanciful as fairy tales told to children. It seemed the stories could originate almost anywhere, with anyone, no matter how questionable the authority, and still be believed by the Spaniards.

The Seven Cities of Cíbola is a perfect example of the Spaniards' failure to question the authenticity of these stories. An Indian slave named Tejo, servant of Nuño de Guzmán, governor of New Spain, claimed to have seen the Seven Cities as a boy. According to his account, these cities, each as large as Mexico City, lay some forty days' ride across a huge desert to the north. In 1531, Nuño de Guzmán set out to find them. He discovered nothing more than the poverty of the northern tribes.

Nuño de Guzmán's failure did not, however, put the matter to rest.

Tejo's story remained alive because it somehow lent support to an old legend of seven bishops who set sail from Portugal and settled the Seven Cities of Antilles. And in due time it was further corroborated by the reports of Álvar Núñez Cabeza de Vaca, who, as treasurer for Pánfilo de Narváez, had gone on the 1528 expedition into La Florida in search of the apocryphal gold at Apalachee. Later, after an eight-year trek and an incredible series of mishaps on his way from Florida to Mexico, he heard in the vicinity of present-day El Paso talk of certain rich cities somewhere to the north. When he related this information to Antonio de Mendoza, viceroy of New Spain, it added credibility to the Seven Cities stories and resulted in even more futile expeditions by the Spaniards, the best-known of which were those of Fray Marcos de Niza and Francisco Vásquez de Coronado—fruitless in their efforts to turn up treasure, but rich in the vast territory they opened up.

The fertile imagination of the Spaniards was hardly limited to the Seven Cities of Cíbola, Apalachee, or other doubtful rumors of great wealth. Spanish adventurers were convinced that somewhere in Florida was the magical Fountain of Youth; that King Dartha, the giant who resided in Chicora, existed someplace in the vicinity of the Carolinas; that nearby stood Diamond Mountain, said to be set solid with gems. The list is as long as it is strange. Cufitachiqui was the land of pearls, and the bells of Gran Quivira, which we now call Kansas, had been hammered from solid gold. There were reports of a weird race of people who nourished themselves on smells, others who lived underwater like fish; a tribe of baldheaded men roamed an area of California. The stories were not confined to the continent: off the coast in the Pacific rich islands rose up, one where you found only gold and another strewn with pearls.

The dreams of modern wetbacks, are they so different? They are only scaled down—a bit. The United States they have seen in magazine photographs, in films, and on TV, is a wonderland little less fantastic than the Fountain of Youth or Diamond Mountain. And, from the ones who've made it across, found jobs, and brought back money, they have heard stories to confirm these images. Up North, even the houses of the *braceros*, the laborers, have indoor toilets, electric stoves, TVs, and automatic washing machines. *Norte Americanos* all have cars—sometimes two and three.

These views seem simplistic until you have visited the poor Mexican villages or the *ejidos* that have cropped up along the border for—it appears to some people—the express purpose of sending their inhabitants across into the Promised Land of the United States. What sets the wetbacks' dreams apart from those of the earlier Spaniards is that the distance is short and the risk is relatively small in exchange for a better life, or—in some cases—any life at all.

One night I walked out into the high desert country of Arizona, where after a scorching day it is suddenly cool and faintly redolent of the foliage of the dry desert. I was struck by how unchanged this border country has

Magdalena Medrano with Jaime and Dolores, Guadalupe Bravos, Chihuahua

Ejido family near Sonoita, Sonora

been since the Spaniards came through. It is hard country, where the weather is merciless and the land often produces little natural food to eat or water to drink. The Spaniards were the perfect people to conquer it. The Iberian peninsula where they were bred and raised, with its own austere mountainous terrain and high desert plateaus, prepared them for the hardships they had to face. These men, Cabeza de Vaca, Marcos de Niza, Melchior Diáz, Coronado, Alarcón, Tovar, Cárdenas, Espejo, Farfán, Oñate, and others, traveling by horseback, occasionally by water, and often on foot, driven by visions of silver and gold, all left their mark on the land.

That night, I wondered as well about the wetbacks, about the swelling tide of illegal aliens already moving under cover of darkness. Did a few drops of the blood of the Conquistadores flow in their veins? Did it feed their desires and keep them strong? I knew that most often they crossed at night and tried to put behind them as many miles as they could. They traveled in rough country where sudden dark arroyos could open up underfoot and let a person plunge through and into brush and cactus and stones, and where rattlesnakes almost as long as a man and as big around

as a man's wrist could be surprised on an outcropping of stones still warm from the late sun.

If the border is the same in such respects as these, it is different, too. The border today possesses a special life that is different from the life in either country it divides. No matter which flag it flies, the land that lies along the border is another country.

It is a country at war.

At any hour, day or night, winter or summer, the borderlands heave and sigh and move under the press of the fantastic force of this strange war. Cars and trucks and buses pass beneath the watchful gaze of armed Customs officials; arbitrarily, they are waved on or told to pull over so they can be searched. If there is a rule as to whom they will detain, it is not clear from the actual procedure. It is the same with people on foot; they spin the turnstiles, going north, going south. Some are questioned and sent through, others are taken aside and frisked.

Somewhere out in the dark, beyond view of the border stations, on almost any night, you can hear the sound of nippers biting through six

Near Lukeville, Arizona

strands of barbed wire and then the murmur of an engine as an unlighted illegal vehicle slips across—into New Mexico, Arizona, California; in Texas, bodies cut through the waters of the Rio Grande, through the brush and cactus of the deserts—*mojados*, the wet ones, seeking work, honest or not, and sometimes trouble; in the half-light of dawn or dusk, a small plane dips below the reach of radar, skimming the mesquite undetected, its engine laboring to keep a load of contraband kited within what the pilot thinks is the safe zone.

From numerous vantage points, I have observed the flow of life on the border. I have watched tourists invade the curio shops of a dozen cities. I've seen servicemen, salesmen, students, politicians, fathers, and other men hunting the pleasures of the whorehouses in Tijuana, Juárez, Ojinaga, and Piedras Negras. I have watched an army of aliens mass on the soccer field near San Ysidro, waiting for the cover of night to break into California. I've sat near the map kiosk in Nogales, Sonora, and stood beside the turnstile near the old Kress store in Nogales, Arizona, while Mexicans and Americans crossed into foreign countries. I have waited on the banks of the Rio Grande at 2 a.m. and watched as mostly men, but also women and sometimes families, waited until a Border Patrol vehicle was out of sight before they splashed across and their shadowy forms were lost in the cotton fields of Texas. I have climbed up toward Sierra de Cristo Rey and watched through a cloud of pea-green smog as the traffic snaked slowly across the international bridges into El Paso, into Juárez—the endless exchange.

I have made my own crossings to confirm and deny each fact about the border. Caught in a crush of cars, trucks, and buses, going one way or the other, inching along slowly, choking from exhaust fumes, I have been assaulted by the racket of ruined mufflers and car stereos, surrounded by beggers—on crutches, in wheel chairs, on tiny caster-fitted carts for the legless, some of them carrying pictures of their children, their mother, or Jesus to increase the impact of their plea and lend credibility to their pursuit—and approached by peddlers of cigarettes, gum, pastry, fruit, and trinkets.

I have tried to make some sense out of the problems of the border, to get a clear perspective on the official restrictions or the official lack of restrictions that govern it. Always I have ended in confusion.

When I asked one Customs agent about it, he said simply: "It's control out of control. There's just no other way to put it."

Fronterizos, the border people, number in the millions. But any accurate census of the border would be impossible. There is a constant influx of tourists, pleasure seekers, wetbacks, and smugglers. They, too, are part of a population that remains difficult to count. They are all citizens of this strange country. They add to its economy, to its tone, its complexity, and the force of their momentum has been significant in shaping both the border culture and the border mind.

If the border is the natural home of many people—good, honest, hard-

"We want clean elections!!!" Tijuana

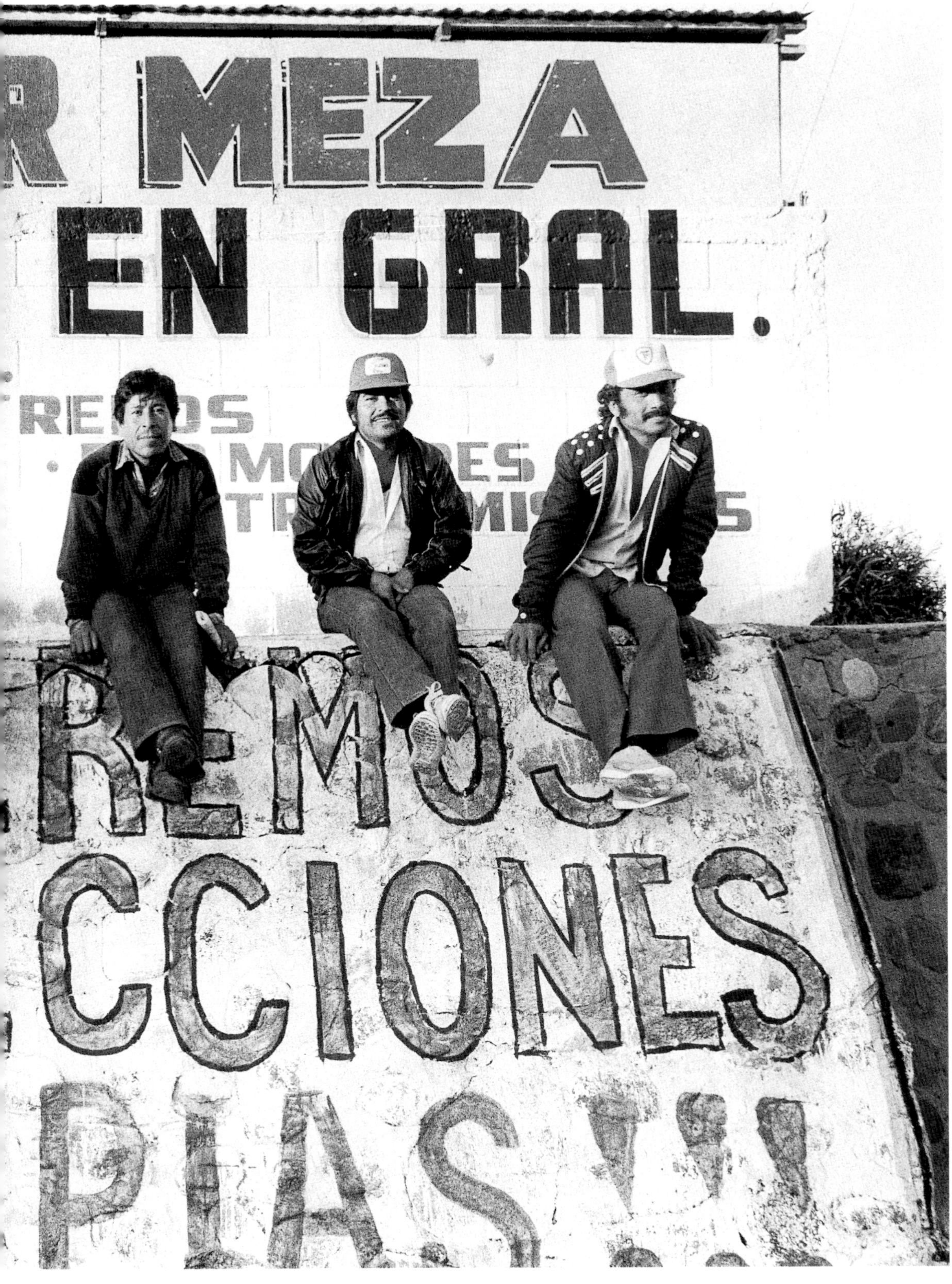
R MEZA
EN GRAL.
CCIONES

working citizens of both countries—it is also a no-man's land for the desperate, a refuge and a hiding place for many more, whose motives are neither good nor honest. Bars, shops, racetracks, restaurants, nightclubs, and businesses hug the line. Pleasure is bought and sold, bartered and taken. Tangible goods are brokered along with lives, destinies, futures. Border-town fantasies inspire countless lost nights away from home, nights of swilling cheap booze, whoring in red-light districts, and searching for the fabled dog-and-pony shows. Texas boys, in particular, have their private stories about the "first time" in the seamy bordellos of their nearest Mexican border town. In parts of the Bible Belt, this is as much a part of growing up as baptism and football.

Much of the life here seems cheaper, rawer, a bit more tawdry. And there is, as everywhere in Mexico, a brazen parody of death, couched in religion and the various forms of magic, that gives it all a special edge.

Tijuana

The beautiful and the ugly stand side by side. Indeed, what appeared beautiful in the glow of last night's neon often takes on a hopelessly drab look in the hard light of day.

One evening I wandered through the dazzle of a carnival at Porvenir. Rides labored on into the late night and barkers competed for the last pesos from families having a big night out; the music ground on and on. I returned the following morning, hoping to photograph the glitter, only to find a decrepit conglomeration of hazardous rides, paint peeling from the ancient wood, the equipment a mess of wire and makeshift patches.

In many ways, life along the border is unique. Juxtapositions spanning a century or more are not uncommon, the result of the clash between the advances of the modern world and of old ways carried over from the past.

Near Guadalupe Bravos, in Chihuahua, I stopped to watch a boy herding goats on a drowsy burro. It might have been a pastoral scene from another time except that he had his ghetto blaster strapped to the saddle

*Piedras
Negras,
Coahuila*

*Maria,
bar girl,
Highway 2,
Chihuahua*

*Carnival,
Juárez*

*Mario Garcia,
carnival,
Juárez*

horn and he was listening to Duran Duran at full volume. The goats, as
indifferent to the loud rock and roll as the burro, munched the strong
grass along the banks of the much-narrowed and deepened Rio Grande,
and the boy seemed transported to a world he could inhabit only in
brief snatches.

Farther south, in McAllen, Texas, on that absolute tabula rasa people
there call "the valley," I met Raul Balli. Raul, who had worked for years as
an employee of Pan American Airlines, had finally come back to the
border. After living in cities like New York, London, and L.A., he had
returned to run his family's business, the oldest tortilla factory in the area.
The place was called El Pocito, the hole in the wall, and it included in
addition to the tortilleria, where many of the tortillas were still patted out
by hand, a flourishing Mexican restaurant that was patronized by a broad
cross section of *fronterizos*, including clients from Reynosa, the Mexican
town across the river.

Raul said he had never intended to find himself running a restaurant
and he sometimes thought about going back to his old job. But in the next
breath he was talking about expanding to a patio, which he showed me,
where people could eat outside on the multicolored *mosaicos*, Mexican
paving tiles.

By all appearances, many border people seem just to have discovered the
wheel. This is not to disparage them; it is simply a fact that the age of
technology, with its incredible power of sweeping change, has been slow
in penetrating the borderlands. A young salesman in El Paso, whose
nametag identified him as J. Rodriguez, smiled at the suggestion. "You see
what they can do with a car. Imagine what'll happen when they get to

Tijuana

computers." I thought it an interesting twist that he was so comfortable using the third person, that his education and job had distanced him from the Third World.

But you do see what can be done with cars. At least half of the visible border industry seems to be devoted to the automobile. *Carrocerias*, mechanic shops, body and fender shops, junkyards, and upholstery shops abound on both sides of the line. Ingenious mechanics dedicate their talents to renovating or tricking out automobiles that are twenty or thirty years old. Day and night you see them being cowboyed together on either side of the border—in shops, under a tree, if there happens to be one, in parking lots, and front yards.

There is a vital rhythm underlying these mechanical trades that carries through the barrios on both sides of the border. U.S. car owners and dealers alike slip across into Mexico to save money on service, upholstery, and paint. If the look of the shops is not always up to American standards, the workmanship is first rate. An ancient generator rewound at a cluttered bench by a man unable to read much more than the "Delco-Remy" on the casing finally works perfectly. A makeshift body shop glows with the sparks from a screaming disc sander as a body man brings a fender back to original shape. Tuck-and-roll tailors may work right on the streets, pulling car seats onto the sidewalk for measuring while an old Singer sewing machine rattles away inside a tiny *tapiceria* shop or under a lean-to, but the covers fit like a glove. Mexicans, able to squeeze an extra

El Paso, Texas

Tijuana

*Vicente Posada
and Gilberto
Lara,
tire repair shop,
east of Juárez*

*Manuel Román
Salazar and
Juan Antonio
Martinez,
Juárez*

decade from their American-made cars, poke through junkyards in the States for parts. The border cowboys, with their homemade hoists and wrenches, team up with *chatarreros* in their junkyards to keep the old tubs running.

"Tub" is not what they call them. These men are connoisseurs of a certain kind of car. "These're the good one's," said one man. "This Chevy, she's a V-8. Nowadays you've got V-6s, if you're lucky. Mostly, you've got them little 4s. And they're dragged down by catalytic converters and shit. And this body," he bangs his knuckles against the fender, "is steel, man, not plastic or some fuckin' kinda tin."

Coming into a border town on the U.S. side, you notice one thing right away: color. It is pure Mexican color, a dazzling play of bright, vibrant hues from a crazy pallette with juxtapositions that should never work and probably wouldn't work in Minnesota or Wyoming. But here they make an uncanny kind of sense. They symbolize the mix that lets it all work.

These hot colors, in combination with cool if sometimes naive design, mirror the climate, the tempo, the spirit of border people, the heart and soul of the land. That, in turn, is reflected in everything else—food, fashion, religion, and music, the brash *norteño* sound that is fresh and different in the way it takes from both cultures.

Border people love the streets. On hot evenings the main thorough-fares open up like communal parlors. People eat at stands—tacos, car-

nitas, burritos, tamales—and drink on the sidewalk. They are gregarious in a way most people in the United States are not.

Border colors, music, cars, language, and attitudes might make you shake your head or smile. But they represent a healthy change after a lot of places, some no farther away than West Texas, where the staid color-lessness of deep-seated conservatism seems designed to keep everything in check, except for those few times when pressure builds and the escape valve blows, causing men to go wild on whiskey, and respectable women to become the subject of ugly rumors. "Plumb loco," is what they say in towns like Marfa and Van Horn. "Damn fool went plumb loco."

The border is a psychophysical warp, like a geologic formation of mind and matter somehow gone wrong. The elements exist in layers, a complex panoply of greed, love, hate, pain. They are like strata that have formed after centuries of filtering down, accumulation, heat, and pressure. No matter how many of them we peel away we are still left with the puz-zling fact that we can't exactly explain this strange and beautiful region that functions as a corridor between the richest nation on earth and one of the poorest.

That single fact, the existence of which overpowers every concrete thing we can hold up to it, has made this strip of land unique. It has brought together each of the elements needed to create an unusual people—the *fronterizos*. And the people are, as they always have been in these parts, the single factor that has made the difference, that has made the border what it is. It is from these people, whose destinies are decided here, that I have drawn the materials for this book.

Sonoita,
Sonora

Handmade
tortillas,
McAllen, Texas

Taquero,
Tijuana

Porfirio Goytia,
La Granje
Mexideli,
El Paso, Texas

El Gato Negro,
bootmaker's
shop, Nogales,
Sonora

*Ubaldo
Montelongo,
headstone
worker, Juárez*

*Pedro
Aquileraa,
master
headstone
carver, Juárez*

Baja California

Near El Paso, Texas

Porfirio
Vargas, shop
owner, Juárez

*Barber in
Palomas,
Chihuahua*

*Police Academy
drill, Juárez*

THE ALIEN

T he door stuck for a second then opened against the wall with a crash. A big rent-a-cop, the fat butt of a .357 Magnum jutting off his right hip, blocked my path. "Pardon me, sir—" he said, roughly pushing my arms up while he proceeded to frisk me carefully, his fingers lingering on the bunch of keys in my pocket, trying to make them for a knife, then slipping down to crush the tops of my boots, where I might hide a gun.

I could have been anywhere in Texas, New Mexico, Arizona, Oklahoma, or Southern California; and, of course, I could also have been in Mexico. This happened to be a rented honkytonk dancehall in a small Colorado town where there were farms and a demand for cheap labor. In the dusty parking lot out front sat a hundred cars, most of which had been carpentered together by the kind of Third World expediency that goes beyond brand-name loyalty and computer-matched paint. Inside, a band from Chihuahua, their Peavey sound equipment fine-tuned and cranked to the max, blasted the room with a relentless hammering of bass, horns, accordion, and guitar.

It was a *fiesta*, the *baile* following a wedding mass at a local Catholic church. The bride had come from somewhere west of Guadalajara, the groom from the state of Sonora. Neither was documented, nor were most of the others who filled the room, including the band. A sudden shakedown by the Immigration people would have produced fewer than half a dozen green cards. The wedding party itself was made up mainly of *mojados*, wetbacks, illegal aliens come to work in this country. They had jumped the border, penetrated the green net of the Border Patrol, and joined the ranks of those who didn't mind doing what one of them called "the shit jobs most gringos refuse to take."

As she danced, the bride seemed glued to the groom. In him was a strength she needed; it was with him that she had realized her dream.

Salvadoran refugee

Juárez

They had had a child before they'd had either the time or courage to celebrate their wedding vows in the openness of a church; and now this little boy, less than two years old, crowded against the snowy lace of his mother's gown and danced as they danced. His problem was different from their's. He had been born in the United States. Technically, he was a citizen. But that would not keep them all from being deported.

The border, with its fences and markers and uniformed officials, with its restrictions and confusion, was a few hundred miles to the south. But it existed here as well, in this hall, in the lives of these people, in this couple and their child. It was as close as the door and the constant threat of an appearance one day by the *Migra*. But that was a fear they had learned to suppress. Now, each time the music stopped and the silence echoed in the room, someone from the crowd came forward and pinned money—good, green U.S. currency—to the crisp lace of the bride's gown or to the dark fabric of the groom's suit. And as they stood there, almost clinging together, they seemed to become symbols of an ongoing struggle that had started with their own ancestors some four hundred centuries before.

The stories were as numerous as the *mojados* jammed into this hall. The bride and groom had come from San Francisco del Rincón and Hermosillo. They spoke of joblessness, poverty, hunger. There were some who had been so frustrated and confused by corruption and fraud that their lives had become impossible to continue in Mexico and Central America.

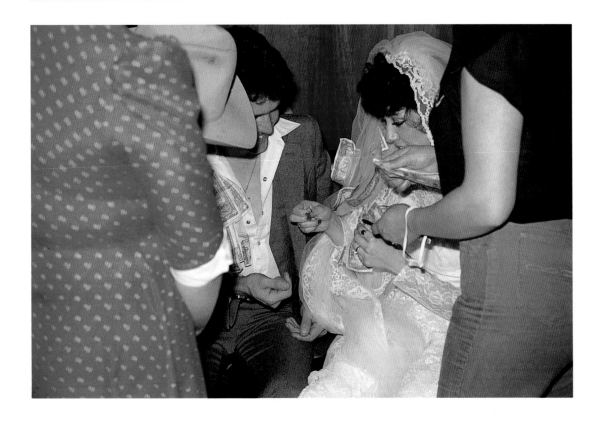

Wedding of ilegales, Colorado

Others had known more immediate pain; they had seen relatives and friends die or disappear; they had fled torture and the threat of death.

At the heart of it all was a deep desperation. The people in this hall and in hundreds of other places in America were survivors from a desperate army of men and women on the march, people who had usually risked everything to get here. Sometimes they made it, sometimes they didn't. They were robbed, raped, and beaten. Sometimes they died. People claimed the death toll was higher than anybody knew. It was, after all, impossible to account for persons whose existence had never been known.

There were stories of children forced to be men and women before they had even reached their mid teens. Sometimes they were slaves. Sometimes they were only kids in a hurry, wanting a chance. Whichever, they were always taken advantage of, pressed into prostitution or made to become *burros* for small-time dealers and pushers. In a bondage of terror, they turned tricks or they taped a couple of kilos of cocaine or raw heroin to their ribs and raced across to drop points in San Ysidro, Calexico, El Paso, or half a dozen other border towns where, if their luck held, they were rewarded with a handful of bills. Sometimes, of course, their only pay was the cold steel shank of a switchblade.

The innocent and uninformed fled north through the Tortilla Curtain, which it is sometimes called and which it sometimes resembles, toward the great nebulous dream they knew as the North. Many of them had

***Illegal aliens,
San Ysidro,
California***

never laid eyes on a map. Some believed, for example, that the entire U.S. border was the state of California. But their ignorance about geography was overcome by sheer will power. How they fixed on a particular destination was finally as frivolous as the decision of tourists who go to Paris to see the Mona Lisa, the only painting they have ever gone anyplace to see.

I saw them on highways, in fields, threading their way through the back streets of cities and towns, like birds whose senses tell them their season has arrived. Once on a West Texas ranch I surprised three kids from Guadalupe, Nuevo León. They were twenty miles inside the United States, not yet out from under the intense scrutiny of the Border Patrol, and wisely kept to the rough and less accessible ranch country. Crouching in the shade of a house trailer, they talked of their plans. One told me he was headed for Victoria, Texas. I wondered why Victoria and was told that there might be work there. A Guatemalan in El Paso said "Mary-land" the way a child repeats a poem from memory. Why? The work would be better farther north. *Verdad?* Another one carefully unfolded a page from a magazine showing the towering buildings of downtown Houston. He looked at it as if it were a shrine.

If any of it made sense, I couldn't see it. I questioned an alien who'd

*Edge of
Border Fields,
San Ysidro,
California*

Texas ranch

lived here for a few years. "No matter what it is," he explained, "it's probably more than they ever had to grasp and cling to before."

Not everyone would agree. In Coahuila I met Alejo Esparza, who had fought in the Mexican Revolution. At ninety, Alejo was out herding his cows. "Mexico is different now," he said. "The young people the age we were during the revolution would never fight for Mexico. They run across the border to live with the gringos. Or they stay here and do nothing."

The border is as elastic as the strange spirit that governs it. It exists to establish the frontier and to limit movement from either side; but, in reality, it stretches to include every illegal alien who has broken through and found refuge in Detroit, Chicago, Minneapolis, Casper, and Seattle.

In many of its aspects, the border is an enigma. It is supposedly governed by a standard set of laws. And that makes it even more difficult to explain how in some places it is a war zone and in others crossing it is no big deal—unless, of course, you insist on making it so. The actual fence is the same. In areas of high visibility it can loom like a wall of steel. But I have driven past miles of border fence in shambles, posts broken or missing, wire on the ground or gone—either stolen or rusted away. In other places, where the fence was relatively secure and whole, I have seen a turnstile built into a corner to allow men from a nearby *ejido* to slip through and labor in the fields of the farmer who paid their wages.

Friends in South Texas spoke of a Mexican woman who, like thousands of others, had waded the Rio Grande each morning for ten years, slipped into the restroom at a fast-food café to change clothes, and came out ready for work. There was another who walked across the bridge every day with a Sears layaway slip and the exact amount in U.S. money to make a regular payment tucked in a pocket of her purse. She went through, worked the day, and returned at night. Customs officials rarely questioned her. When they did, she produced her Sears slip. It seemed they could understand things like layaway at Sears.

That ingenuity is a genuine border product, as real as a piece of garish tourist pottery or a pair of tire-tread *huaraches*. You learn to live along this zone as in a separate country. You learn to make your living or to take your living. And when that becomes impossible, then maybe you do slip into the war zone. Sometimes there is no other way. So it was with Vicente.

I had heard dozens of stories like Vicente's—tales told by people who loved their countries even after being forced to flee them. Vicente never claimed he had been tortured in prison as Jaime had. Nor had he come home one day to find his mother and sister victims of a Death Squad as Roberto had. His house had not been torched, as Jose's had. His job had not been taken, as Miguel's had. But then, Vicente never really wanted to talk about that part, about his reasons for coming to the States, as if the telling might get back, might have devastating consequences for his relatives, his friends.

As the day of our meeting approached, Vicente's nervousness

Alejo Esparza,
revolutionary,
Coahuila

Tijuana

Boy in ejido,
Sonora

increased. The conditions upon which he would see me grew more complex, more tenuous. Over the phone I promised not to reveal the name of the town where he was living, use his own name, or name the country from which he had come. In fact, when I thought about it, I realized I didn't know his country. Looking at his features, when we finally did meet, I might have ruled out El Salvador and might have been wrong in so doing. He could have been Nicaraguan or Guatemalan. I could not tell. But, after all, it didn't matter.

We met in California. The Santa Ana winds had blown out the previous night, clouds the color of steel had settled down to hug the coast,

Children living in railroad car, Sonora

and that entire day had been a deluge. The freeways out of Los Angeles were wet and treacherous, and there was flooding in underpasses and other low-lying areas. The directions I'd been given took me into a lower-middle-class neighborhood, to a six-unit apartment building squeezed onto a small lot on a street of single-family homes. There was a concrete parking lot surrounded by high chain-link fencing; a tricycle lay overturned on a tiny square of lawn; a sandbox had filled with water, a child's toys afloat in it like so many forlorn boats; the stalks of flowers had been broken by the wind and beaten into the grass by the relentless rain.

Vicente showed me into the combination living room/dining room/

kitchenette of a one-bedroom apartment. There were no amenities. Aside from the stove and refrigerator, the furniture consisted of a dilapidated red couch and a straight-back chair. The lighting was basic and harsh, three bare bulbs in ceiling fixtures. Five adults shared this space. All had full-time employment, and most of them worked second jobs at night and weekends. Obviously, money was being saved, either to be sent home or to pay those lawyers who say that for three thousand dollars and a little patience they can guarantee a green card to almost any alien. It seemed that, for these people, everywhere was a new frontier, another barrier.

Vicente directed me to the straight-back chair. He locked the door and then perched on the couch. He began talking immediately in very rapid Spanish. There were a few things about him that I needed to understand. "To start with," he began, "my intentions never were to come to the United States. I didn't plan it. It just happened, the result of circumstances."

He had spent years working for a Japanese company, earning less money in a year than he could earn here in a month—even at substandard wages. He saved for twelve years in order to get his own business. The business he finally bought foundered along with his country's failing economy, barely survived an election, and then it went into even worse times, until Vicente decided he had better sell while he could still recover some of his investment. With his money again in the bank, he was exploring the possibility of starting something new and facing a discouraging set of prospects, when a friend showed up at his house one night.

"My friend had his passport and the necessary papers to go to Mexico. From there he wanted to cross the border into the United States. All he lacked was money, a few hundred dollars. He kept telling me how life was in the United States, how you could work and earn a real living. My friend had a cousin in Pomona, California. He told me about letters she had written. The United States sounded fantastic. But that was the first time I had thought about the United States, and I said no. Still, the more I tried to figure out how to get a new business started or thought about going back to work in my old job, the better my friend's stories sounded, and I decided I had to do it.

"In my country, when you have money things can happen much faster. Normally, it takes a long time to get a passport and the papers you need to travel. But if you can just slip a little money under the table to the right people, they will rush things for you. I paid and paid under the table, and within fifteen days I had my papers."

The fierce rain drove at the building and lashed against the cheap aluminum-framed windows. Vicente pulled his legs under him on the couch, as if suddenly he felt the cold. "Three of us—my friend, his friend, and I—flew to Mexico City on the twentieth of November, which is a big holiday in Mexico. Immigration checked our papers. They went through our suitcases and clothing, looking for drugs. They detained us until we slipped them a little money. Then, of course, everything was okay. We could go.

*Nogales,
Sonora*

"We remained in Mexico City for a couple of days, trying to contact this cousin in Pomona. We acted like tourists, going out to see the sights, the churches, the pyramids. Finally, we reached the cousin and were instructed to meet four other people. That Monday the seven of us took a flight to Tijuana.

"We arrived in the evening, and again Immigration examined our papers and luggage. But these guys were meaner. We were pulled to the side and frisked. Then one of them told us that we were not supposed to be there because our visas were good only as far as Mexico City. We knew this was not true. They asked if we were planning to jump the border. Of course we said no, that we were only on vacation. Then they separated us and tried to scare us. Finally, this one guy turned to us and said, 'Okay, we know you're here to jump the border. That's okay as long as you tell the truth. If you don't we're going to send you back to Mexico City.'

"I told them we were only traveling. We just wanted to see Tijuana. But they knew what was up, and with the Mexicans everything always comes down to how much money they can make. They want to get all they can. The guy who had done most of the talking said, 'If you want to get out of this airport you've each got to give us two hundred dollars.' It was that clear-cut. Either we paid or they sent us back. We talked among ourselves. We had come this far; we weren't turning back. We pitched in one hundred dollars each, and they let us out."

A car drove in, its tires whispering across the wet asphalt. A door slammed. Vicente stopped talking and listened to high heels clacking across the concrete, up the stairs. He got off the couch to unlock the door. A short, very pretty woman came in; she had that doll-like face of Central American women, features that make you judge them to be years younger than they are. I shook her hand. She smiled and disappeared into the bedroom. For the first time, I heard other voices back there.

"Okay," Vicente resumed, "so we took a cab into Tijuana and found a hotel. The change of climate was incredible. It was midsummer when we left home; here it was freezing cold. As soon as we were in the room, my friend called his cousin. She said she was making arrangements with the same coyote who had taken her across. We were to wait there until someone called. We stayed in the room until the middle of the next day, believing it would all happen fast. Finally, we left my friend and went out for food. When we got back he said that the coyote had called. Everything was arranged. We were to meet the coyote in the park next to the hotel.

"We went to the park, but no one approached us. It was frustrating. We waited two hours, moving to different areas of the park, and then we went back to the room. The phone rang. It was the coyote. He said he had been studying us, making sure we would be okay to take. We were to return immediately to the park and talk. My friend asked what he looked like. He said he could not tell us that, but we should not worry—he knew what *we* looked like."

The scene unspooled in my head like a clip from a documentary: the

Central Americans in the United States

seven small Central Americans—cold, apprehensive—creeping back into a scruffy little park teeming with Tijuana street people. I could see the coyote, too, a wily kid of barely eighteen in his short leather jacket, dark aviator glasses and Adidas, pushing away from the tree against which he'd been leaning and watching his new bunch of *pollitos*. He muttered "*A la chingada—*" to himself and gave them a heartless signal of recognition.

One night in Henley's Restaurant in San Ysidro, California, I had approached a few of these coyotes. They were hanging out at the end of the counter, talking in twos and threes and vaguely watching a TV tuned to a station beamed out of Tijuana. This was the United States; but that

Tijuana

was only a fact of geography. I was the only gringo. These guys were going about the business of making arrangements, making deals to pay off the people who needed paying. My presence brought silence, and my inquiries mostly blank stares.

As Vicente described it, this meeting in the park was very formal, with the exchange of names and handshaking, the polite way things are done by Spanish-speaking people. However, when they got down to business, the coyote insisted they leave everything behind in the hotel—everything, including their clothes. He promised it would all be sent over in a day or two.

"My first thought was that the coyote was a flake and trying to steal everything. My friend said he couldn't be. Hadn't he taken his cousin across? Still, that was when the emptiness really hit me. It had been bad enough to leave the things I had at home, where there were relatives to look after them. Now my life had been reduced to what I could carry on my back."

Vicente clasped his hands and put them to his chin. He blew out air, making his mouth sound like an escape valve. "What we did not know was that our calls to Pomona had gone through the hotel switchboard. Somebody had been listening, as they probably did to many of these calls, and this coyote had come through that party, not through the friend's cousin. And of course we never did get our things, including passports and travel documents. They are floating around the black market somewhere.

"We agreed to his terms. They were strict, and we were made to follow them to the letter. We had to walk two blocks behind him. The sun was starting down and the shady streets were beginning to be cold. We wanted more clothing, but it was in our luggage in the hotel. The coyote was already out in front, leading us through the streets of Tijuana, and we had to go on.

"We were made to walk up this long, incredibly high hill. On the other side of the hill we met up with another coyote and a group of fifteen people. The two coyotes had a private conversation. Our coyote came back and said he wanted to let us go with this other group. We said no. We had started with him and if he expected to be paid he would take us across."

Listening to Vicente talk, his voice punctuated by the sound of sheet after sheet of rain driving across the parking lot and spraying against the windows, I pictured the spot he was describing. Only two nights earlier, in fact, I had sat in a Border Patrol truck and watched while hundreds of "*pollos,*" as they were called, staged along that section of the border, were waiting for darkness to make their dash through the fence and into the United States. When I asked to be taken closer, the agent shook his head. "No way. They'll start throwing rocks at us." The Border Patrol, too, waited for the magic cover of night—or at least for the bunches of people to be small enough to handle.

"The group of fifteen went one way. We went another. We walked for a long time, but we could still make out the other group. Suddenly I saw a light in the distance. I called to the coyote. 'You're right! Shit, man—it's the *Migra*. Get down!' We ducked into the tall grass, pressing against the cold dirt. I was scared they would hear the pounding of my heart. The truck drove past, fanning the area with a spotlight. Then it stopped. The larger group had been caught. We saw it. Our coyote kept telling us to keep down. He told us to pull up grass and cover ourselves."

The Border Patrol would have known they were there, somewhere. The night I spent on that no-man's-land, I had been allowed to scan the hills with a sophisticated infrared tank scope mounted on the back of a pickup truck and had been able to make out, in pitch dark, the movement of bodies as they surged deeper and deeper into the hills of California, each one a tiny white figure on an acid green screen. And I watched while this strange, almost unreal game of cat and mouse was being played.

"It must have been half an hour that we lay there without moving— except to get more grass to cover our bodies. The other group was loaded and taken away. One of the trucks came toward us, a loudspeaker blaring: '*Mojados*, wetbacks, come out. We know you're there.' "

He laughed and shifted on the couch, clasping his knees with his arms. "What was really funny was I didn't know what he meant. I had never heard the word *mojado* used like that. I didn't know what a wetback was. None of us moved. We were frozen to the ground by fear. They must have radioed to headquarters because, a few minutes later, we heard a heli-copter. Then suddenly the area was lit up like daylight with a powerful light, and the helicopter swept over us. Our coyote started yelling: '*No se mueven!* Don't move! Cover yourselves with grass!' "

I had not seen that particular piece of ground from a helicopter. But I had been up in one to watch while a rancher shot coyotes that had been killing his sheep and knew how clearly visible everything became from the air. But I had spoken to the Border Patrol pilots. One evening, before they lifted off from the airstrip near the Border Patrol station up on Otay Mesa Road, the Border Patrol pilots had gone over their chopper with me. It was a compact ship made by Bell and assigned to their operation after its service in Vietnam. They showed me the heavy steel wire cutters that had recently been installed above and below the cockpit. Flying mostly in the dark, as they did, ducking and diving over the rough terrain, you could never be certain a set of power lines might not loom up suddenly in their path. That image, along with the framed photographs of wrecked Border Patrol aircraft that hung in their offices, stayed with me as they talked about their trips over the infamous country that lay along the border— Deadman's Canyon, Spring Canyon, E2 Canyon, Washerwoman's Flat.

There were two pilots. One flew the ship while the second operated the searchlight, with its handle that extended down from the cockpit to four quartz lights clustered in a square under the belly of the little ship. "A couple of hours of this shit," declared the second pilot, "trying to keep that light focused down there when you're traveling about sixty miles an hour is real torture to the arms. It's like you've been in the gym all day."

Vicente paused and sat quietly, his arms still clasping his knees. "It is so simple to sit here and tell you what I went through down there, to just be calm and comfortable. But going over it in my mind right now, remembering all the trauma I was going through, remembering the fear and the cold, gives me chills. It seems like just yesterday, but it was two years ago."

He sat stiff and unmoving for a moment, then gradually relaxed enough to go on. "The helicopter kept going around and around. The coyote crawled back and said to wait until it started to go away and then one of us was to run to a tree we could see on the horizon. He said we had to run for our lives. So each time the helicopter would pull up to avoid the hills one of us would break and run. Remember all the hubbub about the track runners at the Olympics? If those judges had seen us running that night they'd have given us more than a gold medal. It is the only way I can explain how we reached the tree safely. My friend fell on the rocks and cut his hand, but that was the only mishap. He wrapped his hand in a handkerchief and we kept going. We walked and walked, and it kept getting colder and colder.

"The coyote led us down to a kind of tunnel. But right at the entrance lay a rattlesnake. We jumped the snake one at a time. Why it never struck one of us I don't know. Maybe it was the cold. None of us would have gone near that snake if we'd had a choice. But by then we had been through so much that a snake seemed like nothing.

"The only light we had in the tunnel was from the matches this coyote had, a small box of stick matches. Just past the snake, he lit one. We were all stopped there, gagging from the smell of sewage coming out of the tunnel. The coyote tied a bandana over his nose and mouth. He asked which of us was the strongest. My friend said he was. 'Okay then,' said the coyote, 'you'll have to carry me through this.'

"The coyote was a kind of prima donna. So, of course, he stayed dry at all times. He just went through the tunnel on my friend's back, lighting matches and holding them until they went out. We came out in a place where there were a lot of houses. Dogs started barking. The coyote said not to move, he would be back."

Was he describing one of the sewer openings I'd been shown? I recalled seeing one near to a subdivision of middle-class housing. The agent and I slipped down an embankment from his truck only to discover a grate of steel re-bar over the opening. The grate delighted the agent. "You can't imagine how I hate chasing a bunch of aliens down into one of these sonsabitches. They stink, and they're dangerous as hell." He set his foot against one of the steel bars and tested it. "You never know if they're going to be armed or not. They're like frightened animals. You don't know what the hell they'll do if you get them in a corner. They could pick up a rock and crush your skull."

Vicente continued his story: "The coyote was gone a long time. We were beginning to believe he might have abandoned us, when he returned and said it was okay to go on. We walked to a freeway, climbed over it, and started up a steep hill. The grass was slick, and we were so exhausted we kept slipping and falling back down the hill. Finally, we did make it. Now we could see the streets of a town, which I later figured out was San Ysidro. Once again, our coyote said we were to wait and follow him at a safe distance. He was always protecting himself. He was no dummy. If they were going to catch us, he was just going to slip away. He led us to a motel. We went in through the back way and directly to a room. He said to wait, he would return. We were wet, and our clothes smelled like shit. We wanted our suitcases. He said they would have to be brought from Tijuana tomorrow.

"We were all men, so we decided just to strip down and wash the clothes we had. We had them hung up to dry and were relaxing when there was a knock at the door. It was the coyote, telling us we were going to have company. Eight more people, men *and* women, were stuffed into the room with us. We were embarrassed and offended that they would put women in with us when we were naked. They had absolutely no respect for *seres vivantes*, human beings. So we dressed in wet clothes. It was crowded; everybody was tense and tired and in a bad mood. There were only two beds, so we let the women have them."

It was the coyotes' way: keep it simple, keep it together. In a motel room in Van Horn, Texas, I listened late one night while a couple of vehicles pulled up. The door to the next room was unlocked, and people could be heard going one after another into the room. Babies began crying. The shower started and stopped, started and stopped—on and on into the night. There were sounds of the furniture being rearranged, mattresses dragged off the springs to make more sleeping room. Finally, everything was quiet except for the occasional crying of a child. I was leaving early. And, in that half-dark, I watched as the room emptied, Mexicans being hurried into the backs of two mud-spattered 4 x 4 pickups with camper shells. It was like one of those circus gags where you watch with increasing disbelief as a seemingly endless number of clowns disappear into a tiny Volkswagen.

"We figured we were in the United States now. All the things in the room were written in English. And the streets we had come through seemed much different from Tijuana. Still, we knew we were not safe yet, and we had no idea when that feeling would come. The coyote came back in and got everybody quiet and said he wanted the money now. My friend's cousin had told him we should pay nothing but gasoline money until the end of the trip. We said no money. The coyote knew this, of course; he, or the person from the hotel, had listened to the phone conversations. So he said he had the car and he needed money to buy gasoline. We asked how much. Three hundred dollars each, he said. We knew that even in America gasoline couldn't cost that much. My friend took me into the bathroom for a talk. We decided we had to pay the guy something. We backed the coyote down to one hundred dollars each, with the understanding that it had to come out of the three hundred and fifty that we were to pay for being brought across. He took that and said he would be back with the car.

"We never saw the first coyote again. He was, it turned out, the brother of the real coyote, the one we were eventually to deal with. He had been gone for a few hours when another Mexican, one we had never seen, came in. We told him we were hungry. He said okay, but he needed money to buy the food, ten dollars each. After a few minutes he returned with two barrels of Kentucky Fried Chicken.

"They kept us in this motel for three days without being allowed to go out. We were brought only one meal a day, and it was usually the same thing, Kentucky Fried Chicken."

One meal a day, cooked and delivered, was luxury treatment in comparison to the circumstances in which many people I'd interviewed had found themselves. Carlos Trujillo, who washes dishes in Amarillo, Texas, told me of a trek he took with two other men from the badlands of Chihuahua into West Texas. At one point they had gone five days without food. They found a flock of sheep and killed one with a pocketknife. None of them had matches for a fire, which they probably would not have dared to make anyway. So they cut off chunks of the warm flesh and ate it raw. They carried pieces of raw meat with them, eating it until the smell was so bad they could not stand to put it in their mouths.

"I didn't know it then," Vicente said, "but the fourth day, the day we finally got out, was Thanksgiving. Because of the holiday it was a good day to travel. Three vans pulled up in front of the door. I had assumed we were the only ones of us in the motel. But it seems that there were at least five or six other rooms just as full as ours—all with the one coyote.

"They moved us into these vans like cattle. It was a modern-day version of the old slave ships. They put only men in the van with me, but we were packed in like sardines. It was even more degrading treatment than we'd gone through in the room."

Everything Vicente said fell into place with all I had learned of the intricacies of the fugitive border. Late one night a Border Patrol agent pointed out the kind of van the smugglers liked best. This particular rig was a yellow Ford that had been jacked up and fitted with air shocks, so that when it was loaded it barely settled down to a normal level. As we watched, gradually getting closer, its driving grew more erratic, and the agent decided to pull it over. He called in the aid of a backup vehicle, and the two forced the van to the side of the road. The driver and two others from the front seat leaped out and fled into a dark field, knowing the Border Patrol would stay with the vehicle. The agent had been right. The van was packed with wall-to-wall wetbacks. There was a crush of men, women, and children, including two babies. Terrified of the lights and commotion, the babies began howling.

"The driver of my van was an American woman. She had a companion, a young man who told us there was heavy control in the San Diego area, so we were going to take a different route. It was a bumpy dirt road, which the driver took so fast we kept hitting against each other. At one point the young guy called out that we were going to pass through a military area, that we should not be frightened.

"All of a sudden we came to a stop. A soldier with a gun stood in front of the van. He talked with the driver. He stuck his head inside and looked at us. We were all dying of fright, knowing we had been caught. Then he just let us pass. We figured it was like Mexico—the guard was a part of the operation, in on the money.

"From that point on, everything went smoothly—except for one incident. Two of the men had been through this before. They kept checking to see where we were. Finally, when we pulled up at a red light in a town, they jumped out and started running. One of the other vans was right behind us and it took after the two men. The guy with our driver pulled a pistol from under his jacket and kept it in his lap, ready to use. You could feel the fear spread back through the vehicle. We kept driving for another hour and arrived at the coyote's house. The other vans were pulling up behind us and, with them, was one of the two guys who had run away. The coyote was furious with him, saying that he could have blown it for everyone. He separated him from the rest of us, telling him that he would find out what was in store for him. That was the last I heard of him.

"Before we were allowed to make our calls to be picked up, the coyote wanted his money—three hundred and fifty dollars. We explained that we had given the first guy one hundred dollars and that all we owed was two hundred and fifty. The coyote said he didn't know anything about the hundred dollars; no one had given it to him. In the end, the brother was brought in. At first he denied having taken the money, then he finally admitted it, and the coyote accepted the two hundred and fifty dollars.

"Then we started making our calls. However, the coyote wouldn't let anybody be picked up at the house, which was a big place in the country. Other arrangements were made—the parking lots of grocery stores, malls, cafés, any place that was safely away from where we were.

"My friend and his friend and I were picked up in a movie theater by his cousin from Pomona. Those first days in Pomona were pure heaven. I had just survived this horrible ordeal, and I was suddenly being fed and treated like a king." He had relaxed, leaning back on the couch, as if it were a relief to relive that moment.

I thanked him for telling me the story and reached to turn off the recorder.

"No, wait—" He held up his hand. "There's more, there's more. It wasn't until a few days later that the real problems came: What was I going to do now that I was here? Where was I going to live? What work was I going to do? Those things were real enough. But the thing that bothered me most is hard to put into words. It has to do with the change. Not just in finding jobs and things like that; you expect problems there. It is

Family in Tamaulipas, Highway 2, Mexico

the attitude of the people toward you and your own attitude toward what is happening to you. You miss everything. You miss your family, your country, your old way of life. It is very different from the life here.

"Working here is also very hard for us. The first thing is the language barrier. Through the help of my friend's cousin, I finally got a job. But it wasn't easy, and it hasn't been easy. Because I am illegal, they expect me to be a slave and to love it. I leave for work at five-thirty in the morning, and sometimes I don't get home until eight at night. They want me to keep

up the pace of a machine. There are no breaks and no real time off for lunch. I can eat lunch, but I have to do it while I am working, a bite at a time. There is a quota for each worker, and if you don't meet it you are fired. I have to work half a day on Saturday as well. That is the reason I have never really mastered English. When I come home at night I am too tired to study. All I want to do is sleep.

"Of course I don't need English at work—except to try and get a better job. All the foremen are Latinos, mostly bilingual Mexicans. They're the worst kind, because they have that one step up on you, and they love to use it to abuse you verbally. Right now my foreman is trying to pick a fight with me. I think he wants my job for someone else. Maybe he has a deal with some coyote. That happens. But, you know, I can stand up for myself without fighting. I'm good with words.

"And I'm lucky. I know that. I have a job, and the money isn't bad. I live here with my family and the others, and it is very harmonious—the way we live in this house.

"Still, I don't know how long it will last. I live in fear of the *Migra*. Who knows how it might happen. That *cabron* of a foreman might blow the whistle. Something. I had a friend here who thought he was home free. One day they picked him up on the street and took him away. He's at the detention center over in El Centro."

In New Mexico, four hundred miles up the Rio Grande from the border, I hear of the exploitation of aliens. Low wages, long hours, and poor conditions are most common. These are minor problems. There are employers who hire a crew of wetbacks for a week to do a hard-labor job. Then, as the crew is finishing up and about to be paid, the Immigration people show up, as if on cue, and haul them away. There are women forced to submit to the fantasies of their employers—either that or be turned in. Once in a while a body is found, a Mexican national—presumably—with no identification. Sometimes there is an investigation.

"I came here," Vicente says, "because it looked like a way out. But I don't want to stay in the United States. Someday I want to go back to my own country. I am not alone. There are a lot like me. We talk about it. We only want a chance."

THE PRIEST

1 waited outside of Casa de Guadalupe for Father Tony Clark, who had invited me to accompany his boxing team over into Mexico to watch them work out at the Centro Desportivo Pedro Gonzalez. Father Tony had begun taking his team across the border after the city of Nogales, Arizona, had condemned and then closed up the building they had been using as a gym. Ignoring the sign and the locked door, the young boxers had persisted in sneaking in at night through a second-story window. Finally, the authorities had cracked down and boarded the place up. A less motivated man might have bowed to those forces; but Father Tony was determined to find another place to train—even if, as he said, it meant taking his team out of the country.

Our seven o'clock departure time arrived, and still Father Tony hadn't shown up. Others were waiting, too. One boy stood on the steps of the house. Occasionally he would face the wall and spar with the shadow of his body cast there by a light from the street. A family had parked their Pinto station wagon in front of the house. The mother and father listened to a Mexican radio station and necked in the front seat while the kids scuffled in the back.

Suddenly, a few blocks to the east, a set of yellow headlights flashed around the corner and swung into focus. A pickup, running badly, lurched and stalled its way up the street. Father Tony leaned from the window and waved. He kept revving the engine while the kid riding with him leaped out and threw open the hood. The Mexican man in the Pinto dug a flashlight out of his glove compartment and crossed the street to peer in at the engine.

The problem was the carburetor, which was leaking gasoline.

"Think you can fix it?" Father Tony questioned the man with the flashlight.

"Maybe—" the Mexican shrugged. Already he had a screwdriver out.

Leaving the man to fiddle with the carburetor, Father Tony took me

Father Tony and Los Guadalupeños

across the street to Casa de Guadalupe. I waited in the living room while he rummaged in other areas of the house for the team's equipment. On one wall was a drawing of Father Tony in trunks and gloves, squaring off, leading with his left, looking stylish and strong. It seemed an appropriate pose for this unusual priest.

Earlier that same day, in Tucson, I had met some of the defendants in the Sanctuary trial. The whole thing had seemed a bad joke, a mockery of those freedoms we'd always assumed were ours. Here were people denied the right to cite their religious and humanitarian beliefs as a part of their defense. Their lives and the lives of thousands of others would be affected by this government's decision.

In Father Tony Clark's face, especially, I had seen something that made me want to know more. And, during the first few minutes of talking in his office behind the Sacred Heart Church, he had put into a capsule his work here, where he had followed his convictions, living the gospel in which he believed and for which he was now on trial.

"I am a priest from Davenport, Iowa. Around 1980, I was invited by Father Vicente Lopez to come work with him in the Diocese of Tucson, in south Tucson. The idea was to live with the people. So we took over a small *capilla*, or chapel, and attempted what we call community development. We were not only concerned with the spiritual well-being of the people we were there to serve but also their temporal well-being. What I mean is if they had roaches in their houses, so did we. If their toilets backed up, so did ours. Our landlords were their landlords. We shared experiences with the people. This was a good program, but it came to an end when Father Lopez was asked to go to Washington to become associate director of the National Hispanic Office of the Council of U.S. Bishops. When he left, I was invited by Monsignor Oliver, the pastor here at Sacred Heart Parish of Nogales, Arizona, to become the Youth Director, which is my position at the present time."

Outside, the truck engine came alive again; it ran a little smoother now. Father Tony paused and cocked his head appreciatively. "Okay, okay—"

He had changed into a natty golf cap and a satin jacket emblazoned with the name of the boxing team: *LOS GUADALUPEÑOS.* He gathered up a ghetto blaster and a couple of large containers of equipment the team would need. He threw the stuff in the back of the truck. A kid in a sweat suit was coming down the street. Father Tony stood out on the running board and yelled: "Come on, come on. We gotta hustle—"

Hearing nothing in his voice that sounded like Iowa, I asked where he'd grown up.

"Pennsylvania—York, Pennsylvania."

Perhaps that explained the tough, pugnacious exterior, even the boyish charm that lurked behind his dark smile. A certain working-class savvy was there in the body, in the attitude; and down here on the border it gave him a license, a strong credibility.

Father Tony training a fighter

He started the engine. It ran better now, but it was far from perfect. The cab still smelled of gasoline, a reminder that the problem was much more serious than a flooded carburetor. The thing ran in furious fits and starts, shooting ahead, then ducking and diving and threatening to quit. It threw us back against the seat and forward against the dash. Father Tony never stopped the pickup completely; he slowed only enough to let members of the team run alongside and leap into the back.

Predictably, a long line of vehicles waited at the border station. Father Tony shot along one side of the line of cars until he was at its head. He leaned out of his window, extending both arms, and pleaded with the lead driver to let him slip in, all the while having to pump furiously at the accelerator to keep the engine running.

The Mexican customs official recognized the father and waved him through with the kind of bowing move that a matador might make with his cape. The condition of the engine was deteriorating rapidly. At any moment I expected fuel to splash onto the manifold; there would be a cloud of smoke, and flames would come licking out from under the hood. But the thing kept going. We picked up more kids on various corners in Mexico. The boundaries of Father Tony's parish, it seemed, extended to anyone who wanted or needed his help.

The engine died while we waited for a traffic light. Father Tony got it started. It began cutting out in the middle of the next block. The truck jerked on to an intersection and then quit when Father Tony failed to out-bluff a Mexican in a cattle truck. He ground and ground at the starter. It wouldn't catch. We sat there for a minute.

"Maybe God's trying to tell me something," he said, his eyes sparkling.

He tried again; the engine fired. We shot ahead, turning up a long slow hill that eventually led to the gym. The pickup faltered, gasped, and died. There was something final in the way it stopped: stone cold dead. The street was full of traffic. Cars were trying to squeeze past—honking,

waiting. We all piled out and began pushing while Father Tony steered the pickup into a parking space in front of a *cervezeria*.

This was a story of a priest on the border during a strange, sad war. During the morning he was on trial; the outcome of that trial could either see him acquitted or thrown into prison. The rest of the time he spent working. This was a typical night in his life. His job was youth, and he didn't do it according to any standards set out by church authorities in some isolated office somewhere. He did it according to what he saw and felt was needed, and he was gratified that it came with the blessing of his pastor.

"On the border here," he had informed me earlier in the day, "there are a lot of street kids. We have a large drop-out rate. We have a large number of kids that don't have jobs. This is a very high-profile area, and the statistics speak for themselves. The numbers of drop-outs and jobless, the kids in trouble, are as high as or higher than anywhere else in the United States."

He knew why that was. He had been quick to realize that you could not apply the same treatment here that you might use in Salt Lake City, Minneapolis, or Davenport. "Even though we are in Arizona, in the United States, our particular area is more influenced by Mexico. And I think there

is a great conflict in this. I think the educational system they're trying to use here is imported from the United States. And I think there is a real lack of professional care and—I hate to say this—a lack of interest in responding to the needs of this particular community. The institutions and their efforts to serve the people here lack real understanding and a deep-rooted appreciation of this locale."

Watching Father Tony in that situation, with a broken-down truck, a bunch of disadvantaged kids from both sides of the border, I knew I was witnessing a man who could come up with solutions, who probably even

had the ability to work the small miracles that seemed to be expected of him. He was happy with the challenge he had found. "Yes, I do like it here," he said with a smile. "It is a great ministry. I have a good pastor, Monsignor Oliver, who encourages initiative, who encourages creative responses to people who bring pastoral needs to us and to our community."

Father Tony and I watched two of the boys inspect the leaking carburetor. Was this, I wondered, the creative ministry he had mentioned? Father Tony worked from a new set rules—or no rules at all. It was a challenge that had brought him new insights, new perceptions. "I think

*Conference
room,
Sanctuary legal
headquarters,
Tucson,
Arizona*

every priest should have an opportunity to know a Third World nation or to deal with people from the Third World," he said. "It is amazing how people can come from so much darkness and bring so much light to we who, I think, live in a cellophane bag. We are isolated from so much, protected from so much."

He meant not simply people in general but also the church as a whole. "I think the ministry in the North is stagnant. I think that it's conventional. I think that it is humdrum. And I think that it and the United States in general must be revitalized." He smiled then and his teeth shone beneath his small moustache.

When it became clear that the boys could do nothing for the truck, Father Tony cried: "*Vamos!* Let's hitch a ride."

By all standing in the middle of the dark street, in the late rush traffic, which in Mexico is an act verging on suicide, we were able finally to stop a pickup truck and get a lift up to the Centro Desportivo Pedro Gonzalez.

The building was set back from the road and flanked by two rows of sorry shacks. The outside was dark, except for a square of light where the door stood open. Through it, past the watchman who sat in a silver metal Corona Beer chair, in the dingy interior, was a twice-life-size painting of a fighter, possibly Pedro Gonzalez.

Father Tony was immediately at home, able to ignore the unpleasant smells of sweat, urine, and too much spilled beer. He got his team lined out. They would work for three minutes at a single exercise. Then they would move on. He had a timer set to go off loud enough to be heard over the rock and roll tape on the ghetto blaster. It was an experience to watch him. He was tough; he was perceptive; he was innovative—a professional who understood both boxing and how to get the most out of these kids.

How did it happen that he had organized a boxing team? "Everywhere I have been, I've had one," he declared. "I believe that there is a great need to work with marginal youth. I'm talking street kids. I've found that the most effective way to reach street kids is to meet them where they're at, rather than have them come and try to hold the values and interests that we have. We have to meet on a turf where we can *share* interests and values."

Another person, equally as dedicated, equally as concerned, might have chosen a different sport or no sport at all. But boxing is what Father Tony knew and believed in. "Boxing," he said seriously, "is more than boxing. Boxing is getting kids back to school. Boxing is helping them find a job. Boxing is sharing their plight. But boxing itself holds a lot for them. There is the uniform, for one thing. There is the fellowship. There is the identity, and it is a very positive identity."

That much I had seen. There was a pride in the team, a sense of belonging, a strength. Father Tony had broken through the barriers of culture and class. He was adviser and coach, of course, but he was more. He was a friend; they had met at that level; and it was working.

"There's a big difference between being in a border town and being

fifteen, and being in the midwest United States and being fifteen. A fifteen-year-old here has much more responsibility. He is totally responsible for his own education. He is totally responsible for his spending money. There is no such thing as an allowance. There is no such thing as, Hey, mom, can I buy this, can I buy that? The temptation to steal is almost like, How much should I steal, instead of should I steal or shouldn't I."

Money, too, was included in the education. He saw to it that these boys had an opportunity to work and earn money. A couple of them did odd jobs for the parish. He interceded with members of the congregation and community to get part-time jobs for others. Some of the money was to spend; the better part of it went into savings accounts in their names.

Behind us in the echoing concrete room with too little light and the dank pervasive smell of a sewer threatening to back up somewhere, I heard the rhythmical hammering of the speed bag, the thud of the body bag, the whispering of a jump rope on a floor stained with blood and God knows what else. A boy groaned out the last few chin-ups on a bar, and the buzzer sounded.

"Let me tell you a story," Father Tony began. Then he changed his mind. "No, you can do it yourself sometime. Ask a kid of six or seven what he wants to do when he grows up. He'll tell you: I want to be a pro football player; I want to go to the moon; I want to drive a race car. The sky is the limit. You go into a barrio in Mexico and ask a kid the same question, and he just looks at you like you're crazy. These kids don't think about that. They don't dream like that. They don't know what they want to be. You better ask them what they're going to eat tonight. That's the kind of future they think about. These kids that I'm working with here are prod-ucts of *that* world, *that* thinking."

When three minutes were up again, Father Tony shifted everyone around, keeping the routine on the build. He picked up where he had left off. It was a point he wanted to stress. "They don't look to the future. They don't say: if I do this now it will affect this later on. And yet the deci-sions that they make are really impressive. They are mature and thoughtful. They mature quickly; they have to. If you know Piaget, you'll remember that he says that the criterion of all human intellect is not if-this-person-scores-this-score-on-a-test-at-this-time but how a person is able to manipulate and survive in his environment. If you apply Piaget to the situation here, then these kids are geniuses. I'm with geniuses. And yet they are flunking their subjects. Or they don't go to school at all. They are disorderly, et cetera, et cetera. I say that is *our* mistake, and I'm convinced of it."

He stepped over to a small boy working with a set of dumbbells. He took one of the weights and showed him the correct form, how to hold his back straight, how to direct the work to his arms—where he needed it.

Coming back to where I stood, he said, "The faith in these border kids is very very strong."

"Why do you think that is?" I asked.

The border fence near Sonoita, Sonora and Lukeville, Arizona

Girl selling candy, Sonoita, Sonora

Orphans near Tecate, Baja California

"I think it's because they live so much in the realm of existence. The more you need God, the more you turn to Him, and the more he manifests his presence; the less you need Him and the less you turn to Him, the more distance you find between Him and yourself. It is very important for the people here that the presence of God is manifested daily and in the most ordinary things of life. The churches reflect their community. The problem with most of us is that we live in an age of departmentalism. If I'm sick I go to a doctor. If I want to lose weight I go to a gym. If I want

some spiritual high I go to church. If I do these things on a regular basis then I'm considered normal. Well, I think that's the most abnormal route you can go. It's subductive, its destructive. It's like what they do to people in the prisons. It is so routine that you don't even want anymore. You just eat and sleep." He held up a finger. "But not here. There's not one day that is the same on the border."

The word *prison* had seemed to echo strangely in the gym. And I thought at the time that Father Tony was probably grateful that none of my questions had been specifically about the trial. Nothing had gone well

in the courtroom, and later on it would be worse. I assumed, too, that it was out of relief and appreciation that he had talked at such length about the kids. Had I known Father better I would have realized I was wrong. Because when we did speak of the trial one afternoon in his office he was as open and forthcoming as he had been that night at the gym.

We talked less about his involvement in Sanctuary than about his own feelings for the people who had sought him out and his role in responding to their pleas for aid. On that subject he was unshakable. Their politics were nothing to him. His concern was for their lives.

He could not recall exactly when it had started. "We're not talking about once or twice, not a couple of isolated incidents," he reminded me. "We're talking about a four-year period of involvement. There are two things that have to be held out as denominators, two things that got me involved. First is being on the border; and second is being identified with the Catholic church."

"Why would they single you out?"

"The largest building in this town is the Catholic church. You come across the border or you look into Nogales from those hills over there, and the first thing you see is the church. To these people from Central America the church is the center of the community's life. You have the plaza, and you have the church. You bring that with you when you're

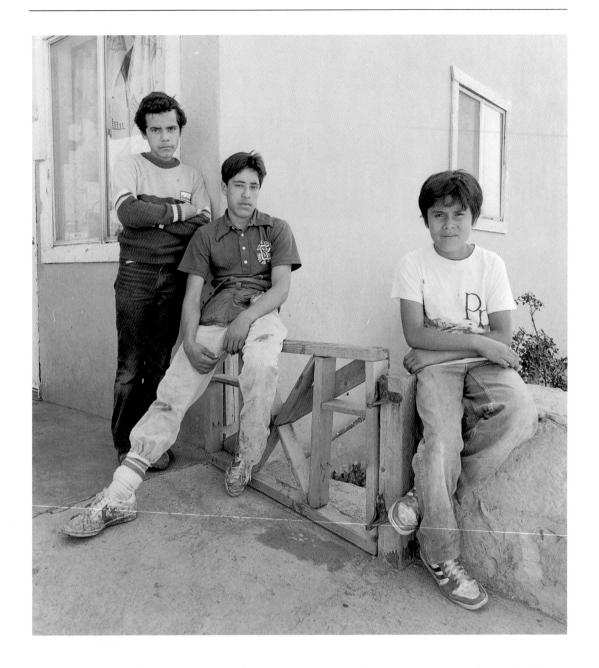

Orphans, Baja California

looking across the border for safety and security, for some kind of refuge, and you're going to gravitate to that church. I would say that is how 95 percent of the refugees found themselves here. So my involvement was easy. I'm stationed. I'm the youth minister. At that time I was still living here at the church. And of course they didn't come at office hours. They came at six in the morning, or they came at ten at night."

He had not advertised. God had advertised—with the cross, with the church. Father Tony served God. He had to respond—not as a criminal but as a Christian, as a human being. He had provided basic things to people in need. The people who impressed him most were those who were really, finally, down and out and desperate.

"What was unique about the Central Americans is that, while a lot of people came and asked for food or they had run out of money or were desperate in one way or another, these people came with all that *plus* stories that would affect anyone with blood in their veins. There were a lot of life or death situations. Most of us Americans think that only happens in movies. You can see it in these people's eyes; you can see it in their faces. These people are genuine—no fakes. Or if they are, then they ought to get an Academy Award for acting."

He had been overwhelmed by the stories of what the refugees had been forced to go through to get there. But he had been moved more by what he had actually seen. The people were walking casualties. Some of the experiences among the hundreds he had heard stood out. He recalled

**Reynosa,
Tamaulipas**

particularly a day when a certain mother and her children presented themselves at the church. He had been in the churchyard with Mary Kay Espi-
nosa, another of the defendants in the trial. "The mother began telling us
she was from El Salvador and that these were her children. All of a
sudden one of the children came up the mother and said—it's time. And
the mother said—no, no, not here, not now. And I said to the mother—it's
time for what? And she said that the child meant it was time to take
shelter from the bombing. They were from San Miguel, and it had been at
that time of day that they all had to get off the street because the bombing
was about to begin. The child was trying to tell the mother that we should

take shelter, that we should hide. I just looked at Mary Kay and shook my head. That's what they were running from. Even though they were removed from the situation by weeks or months, the fear was there, and the child was really upset."

There were stories of the death lists. Families of children were fleeing because their parents had been forced out and they were trying to find them, wondering if they were even alive. Parents were hunting their children, hoping to be united. And then there were the stories of how it was to come through Mexico, the stories of being robbed, raped, being put into jail for no reason except that they were Salvadoran. And there were stories of their treatment in jail.

"Four years of this convinces me that everybody can't be lying. People that don't know one another have the same kind of stories. Even after they had escaped from their own countries, Mexican officials would take them off buses, planes, trains and tell them they had to pay three hundred dollars or be arrested. They would take their jewelry, anything of value."

The whole thing, he admitted, was a learning process. From the side of the church, as he understood it and represented it, he knew what he had to do. But somewhere on the periphery were the law and politics. "If someone says they are hungry, you feed them. If they don't have clothes, you find them something to wear. If someone needs shelter, you find them someplace to stay. Those are the normal things. But if someone comes and tells you I am hungry, these are the only clothes I have, I need shelter, and I can't go back where I came from if I want to continue living, then the situation is no longer normal."

He paused, knitting his fingers together on the top of his desk. "It became clear that the refugee from Central America could not apply and expect the due process of law, as we say. It does not exist. I have evidence of that. And knowing those things, the demands on us were for a much more personal, more committed response. And things like transportation became very important elements in it."

That was as specific as he wanted to get and all he really wanted to say. He was fidgeting, anxious to get to work. He stood up. Then, leaning on the desk, he added this about the people: "They made all the arrangements. We assisted them while they were here. We assisted them in their needs. But they made the arrangements."

He echoed himself, as though in that statement there was some hope. I would not think much about those words until months later, when I heard that Father Tony, along with seven other Sanctuary workers, had been found guilty of conspiring to smuggle, transport, and harbor illegal aliens. Still to come was the sentencing, at least five years in prison and fines up to $10,000. And there would be an appeal.

Reading of the conviction, I found myself remembering his words, bits of our interviews. I remembered him as a man working to build citizens. And it was no real consolation to know that, if he went to prison, he would not find it so routine that he would not want anymore.

THE AGENT

1 learned about Agent Thomas L. Harrison from his son Mike. Like his father, Mike had joined the Border Patrol, something that obviously ran in the family, because Tom Harrison's father had been a career agent back in the days when the agency was still cutting its teeth. Three generations of a single family.

In my border trips I had met a number of other border patrolmen, encountering in the process everything from the Texas Ranger type, with that raw, frontier bravado, to the cooler 007s and supercops armed with the latest technology.

Recalling the film *The Border*, I could easily see both of the characters played by Jack Nicholson and Harvey Kietel as pretty normal border patrolmen. They fit in with the tough, callous, hard-line agents who went at their job with a vengeance, and their much gentler counterparts whose humanity sometimes got in the way of their work. For example, I remember watching an agent in San Ysidro, California, sprinting after a young alien. They went around a motel, into the street, and finally, a block away, the agent threw the alien to the pavement. By contrast, I remember going into the field with an agent who slowed his truck to point out a small farm. "We know the old man here's got a couple of wets," he said. "But he's all crippled up, and his farm would go under if he didn't have them to help." In larger cities, I was sometimes assigned to agents handpicked by the public relations officer; they had a middle-of-the-road speech they gave that was liberal enough for the media but didn't cast a bad light on the agency.

Among them all, the tough, the lenient, Thomas L. Harrison stood out. He was a man of medium height, solidly built, with a strong look of determination and purpose in his face. I do not know what a model agent would be; but if Tom was not one, he was at least his own man. He knew what he stood for and exactly what he would do to enforce those princi-

Thomas L. Harrison, U.S. Border Patrol, Presidio, Texas

ples. Listening to his story was like an informal review of the growth and coming to focus of the entire Border Patrol.

Harrison's office was in a prefab building on the outskirts of Presidio, Texas. The walls were covered in a paneling that had been printed with soft, almost shadowy frontier scenes. Behind his desk was a bookcase filled with manuals, forms, and Spanish dictionaries—everything in perfect order. On the bottom shelf was a blue wooden shoeshine box, which I suspected he used every day.

It was not a private office. And just as I began the interview, a tall, thin agent sat down at the next desk and started cleaning a large-caliber revolver, a .357 or .38 with a four- or five-inch barrel. The radio crackled, and two patrolmen talked back and forth as they closed in on a group of aliens they had located in the brushy hills north of town. Tom turned down the volume and pushed the standing mike away from the middle of his desk, as if to lessen the temptation to join in from where he was.

HALL: How did it come about that three generations of your family have been in the Border Patrol?

HARRISON: During the Depression my father was working for a low amount of money. He was from Paris, Texas, over in Lamar County, and he noticed that government employees were doing better than anybody else. So he aspired to be a railroad mail clerk. There were 2,800 men who took the exam in Dallas. They told him when he passed the test that they would call him. They did call his brother-in-law, who had taken the test the same day. But they didn't call dad.

Then about two years later, in 1938, he got a call from the Border Patrol. They told him his name had been entered on the register and that they were using the same one that had been assembled for the railroad mail clerks. Did he want to be in the Border Patrol? He didn't know anything about the Border Patrol, but he needed a job real bad and they were offering eighteen hundred dollars a year, which was a phenomenal sum in those days.

He reported to duty in El Paso, Texas, in August of 1939, and went through the Border Patrol Academy. When he got out, the Second World War was getting pretty hot. Everybody tried to enlist in the military, but the Border Patrol were frozen to their positions.

The agent cleaning his pistol ran a copper-wire brush through the barrel and then held the piece up to the light to make certain the spiraling bore shone.

HALL: What was the Border Patrol doing in those days? Was it the same work?

HARRISON: No, the problems were a little different. From El Paso they sent dad to Fort Hancock as a supervisor. The agents were picking up people, processing them, and determining what their nationalities were.

HALL: This had to do with the war?

HARRISON: Yes. They detailed him to New York City for nine months. While he was working there, he and a bunch of his peers went down and

Carlos Johnson Gutierrez, Mexican immigration officer at Antelope Wells, Arizona, border crossing

joined the Marine Corps. Before the paper work could come down they found out that once again the Immigration Service had frozen all the supervisory officers. They weren't letting them go into the military.

HALL: What kind of work did he do in New York?

HARRISON: He worked with the Jewish people. The ones that were here were all trying to convert their citizenship to the United States. It was the same with the ones that were fleeing the oppression in Europe and coming in—they wanted citizenship, too. He had to screen those people and determine their elegibility. He did the same thing in his next posting, which was San Francisco. He had to handle the Asiatic people that were being brought to San Francisco claiming oppression from the Japanese armies.

At the next desk, the agent had finished his cleaning procedure and was fitting the cylinder to the revolver. He snapped it into place, took aim out the window, and clicked the trigger. He clicked it again and again, checking the action.

When he finished there they sent him back to Texas, to Alpine, to be an Assistant Chief Patrol Agent. Then, in 1949, we moved over to Marfa, Texas, and by 1951 he had made Chief Patrol Agent. He was in charge of the Marfa Sector, which goes up through Kansas and takes in part of Colorado and the Texas Panhandle.

HALL: At what point did the Border Patrol make the biggest changes toward what it is today?

HARRISON: 1954. Eisenhower was president, and he wanted the entire alien population processed and documented. We didn't have very many people working for the Border Patrol. We had eight hundred men. He pushed it through Congress to double that number. He got us some radio equipment and more or less paramilitarized the Border Patrol. As a part of that push they sent my father down to McAllen as Chief Patrol Agent because they had about 400,000 known aliens in that area. It was a large push. They brought in a lot of investigators and cleaned out the Rio Grande Valley from Laredo all the way to Brownsville. They apprehended more than 400,000 and caused an even greater number to leave voluntarily.

That push lasted three years. During that time we established what we called detention camps along the border. McAllen had one; El Paso had one; and El Centro, California had one. They transferred my father to El Centro, and he ran that sector until 1961. In February he was sent back to Brownsville, which had become the Port Isabel Sector. He was there until he retired in December of 1965.

HALL: When did you join the Border Patrol?

HARRISON: I came into the service in 1961.

HALL: How had it changed since 1939 when your father went in? Was the training more intense?

HARRISON: Almost everything was different, including the training. The training for a Border Patrol officer is rigorous. And even after training, the border patrolman is on probation for years. You have to be in the service three years to get a career appointment. The primary reason we are so hard on our new officers is that every time we go to court and lose a case we lose part of our ability to do our job. You see, we are the only agency I know of in the United States that can arrest without warrant. And when you are dealing with a person's liberty you are also affecting his family.

HALL: How does that affect families?

Tom Harrison's hand had moved to the belt of his holster set, and he played idly with the extra load of six bullets, moving them up and down in their leather loops like the valves on a horn.

HARRISON: These people come over here, they get married, and they have children. When we go and arrest them we separate families. You do a

Mike Harrison,
U.S. Border
Patrol

Columbus, New
Mexico

lot of tragic and traumatic things when you enforce our laws. These are very unpopular with the general public, and the important thing in my mind is that if these officers aren't well trained they will eventually lose all authority to do their job. The famous Miranda decision was against us. We do have well-trained men. I can take two of my officers and send them to New York City, and they can do anything that is in the Immigration book. I myself have been detailed to both coasts and all over the U.S. A border patrol agent is expected to be a unit and to function anywhere, and we always have. All the other agencies know this. The DEA and the FBI take a lot of our officers. Any service that can will draw from our ranks. Its because of training. I'm not talking about book training, although they are fluent in Spanish and proficient in the immigration and naturalization laws. I'm talking about the kind of training that makes an individual self-sufficient.

HALL: Why such intense emphasis on training?

HARRISON: We can't afford to make mistakes. The Border Patrol is a uniformed force, and we have to keep a low profile because the United States has always been worried about a police state. That's why there are very few uniformed, armed federal officers in the United States today.

HALL: I've been told that the Marfa Sector, of which you here in Presidio are a part, is different in most respects from the rest of the border.

HARRISON: The Marfa Sector is entirely different. The Rocky Mountains, the Livermore Mountains, and the Eagle Mountains are large natural barriers that make it necessary for these people coming through here to walk over some of the roughest country in the United States. They have to go two hundred miles to get to the first agricultural area where they could find work. And the people coming in looking for work, which 99 percent of them are, are going to go the easiest way they can. They're going to go to places like the Rio Grande Valley, where they can find work in ten or twenty miles. They're going to San Diego, where they can slip through and hide in Los Angeles. They're not going to come here and walk over mountains that are as high as eighty-four hundred feet. The one you can see right out this window is seventy-seven hundred feet. They're not going to walk over that kind of area for two hundred miles looking for a job when they can take a bus to Juárez or Tijuana and find work in a shorter distance. It's too much effort.

HALL: So you get experienced people?

HARRISON: The people we get are people who know where they are going and who can walk two hundred miles to get there.

HALL: Are many of them moved by coyotes?

HARRISON: We don't have any regular coyotes that cross people here. We are too hard on regular people. There are some organized groups in Mexico, two or three that we know of in Ojinaga that set up loads of aliens going north. They send somebody that knows the way and can drive the cars out. But we've gotten so rough on them that they stay hid pretty good.

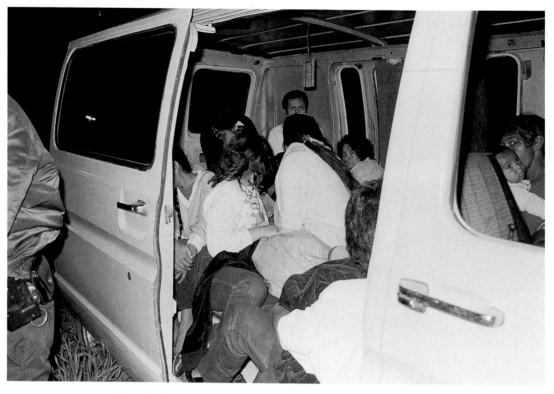

Illegal aliens in van,
Otay Mesa, California

Illegal aliens,
California

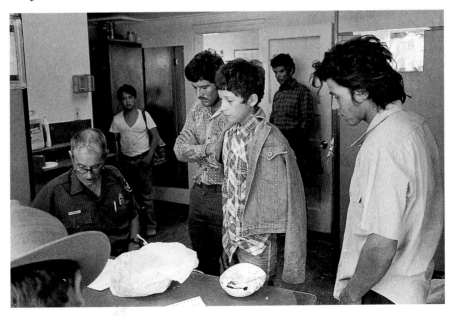

Booking
wetbacks,
Columbus,
New Mexico

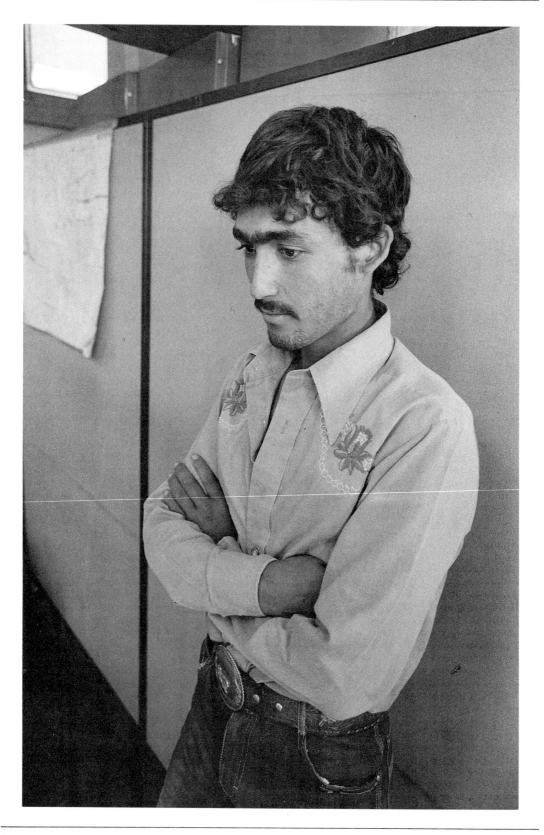

HALL: Do you have agents in Mexico?

HARRISON: We don't do any work in Mexico. This is detrimental to our operation because we should have that intelligence coming in. Other sectors do have a large number of antismuggling agents that work in Mexico and tell their people what to expect. But we don't.

HALL: Does that have something to do with drugs?

HARRISON: Yes. We catch a low amount of drugs—marijuana, heroin, and cocaine; but 90 percent of it is marijuana, and 90 percent of that is like six kilos, ten- or twelve-pound deals in a car, where a guy is just trying to make some extra money. I call big loads in the thousands of pounds, and we haven't caught any of those. We don't get anything like they're catching in New Mexico or El Paso, places like that.

HALL: Is it just not coming out here?

HARRISON: No. There's a large bunch that ship out of Ojinaga, but they do it by air. They just jump over us. The only radar protection we have is in Wink, Texas. Almost anyone can fly out of this area without touching the radar screen. The military is concerned about this. They send planes down here every day to try and hide from their radar in El Paso, which we don't get to use. But they're trying to make sure there are no holes in their radar system. It is a problem for national security as well as narcotics trafficking.

HALL: You have fewer agents than most sectors. Does that mean the risk factor is lower?

HARRISON: We have probably more shoot-outs per alien apprehended than anywhere else. We've had several serious shootings down here; several of our officers have been killed or wounded. In 1982 I had an officer shot up pretty bad over a dope deal. We were notified that aliens were camped on this man's property, and when we went down to investigate it they started shooting. One alien shot an officer before his partner could shoot the alien, which he finally did.

HALL: Why so many shoot-outs?

HARRISON: One reason is there are more firearms here. This country is desolate, and it's full of old-time Texans, and on both sides of the river people are real independent. There's not any law on the Mexican side, and the Border Patrol is about the only law over here. There's one sheriff's deputy here, so we get called in a lot to assist for the sheriff's department. The other night there were some drunks shooting an AR-15 back toward town. There was no sheriff available, so we had to go take the gun away from the guy. Those incidents expose us more than is necessary to do our job. But we have to get along with the other law enforcement agencies. In fact, in Texas it is the law that you have to assist them when they call.

HALL: I have heard of a number of illegals who are working in this area. Is it policy to be lenient about that?

HARRISON: No. We try to get them off. We know they are here, and we check the ranches. But, like everything else, our policies keep us from being too effective. Fifteen years ago we were allowed to work anytime we wanted to, and we were a lot more effective. Now we can't go on a ranch before daylight, and we have to be off before dark. If you know anything about ranching you know that a cowboy is out working before daylight and he's home after dark. The only time we could catch him we are not allowed to be on the place. Now there is a good reason for that: people started shooting at us when we came sneaking up in the dark. They didn't know who we were.

I've been in this area twenty years, and I've caught the same individuals two or three times. There's one fellow I've caught at least three times. But he stays on a mule. He goes and gets his instructions from the boss when there's nobody around and he goes and does his work and he never shows up at headquarters. He's practically impossible to catch. You can't use a helicopter to catch a man on a mule. You can't use a jeep. About the only thing is men on horses, and you have to know where he is to get your horses into that area.

In this rough country its impossible to keep them all caught. We chase people across these ranches, and we occasionally run onto illegals working there. We take in everyone we run into. But they can get by us. There is one ranch that is five hundred square miles under fence. I chase across it every day, and I run into their illegal cowboys. I've had special permission from the chief to go in before daylight and catch them in their sleep. I've only been given that permission twice, and both times I've caught the man. Of course, I can understand the chief's position. If he gives me permission and somebody shoots one of my men, then he's embarrassed by it.

HALL: So they have the advantage.

HARRISON: Yes, and this old rough country is difficult. They can hear a car coming for ten miles, and ten miles in this country is thirty minutes. Anybody that can't get away from you in thirty minutes just isn't trying. If they're out making fence or something, and they hear a vehicle, and they aren't expecting anyone, they know its got to be us. We find lots of abandoned camps, lots of tools. They run off and leave them, and they won't come back. Sometimes when they see our vehicles they just quit and go plumb back to Mexico.

HALL: Is that the most difficult part of your job, then?

HARRISON: No, the paperwork is the most difficult part. It takes about 20 percent of your effort to apprehend people; it takes 80 percent of your effort to process them and write it up properly. The government continuously needs more copies. If you catch an individual with false documents, then there are three places that want copies of that. If you catch a man down here on one of these farms picking onions and he's not making minimum wage, then the Minimum Wage Board in Dallas has to have a copy of that.

For the first time in the interview, Tom seems perturbed. This is obviously a point that gives him a lot of trouble.

There's just a mountain of paperwork. If I apprehend an American

*Border Fields
near San
Ysidro,
California*

*End of the
border, Pacific
Ocean*

citizen and he's transporting illegal aliens, then that is a different set of papers. If he is an armed individual, that is additional paperwork. It's just a quagmire of different forms. Now, to my way of thinking, all the information they request is necessary, but I don't agree with us having to make all these copies.

When my reports go in they want to know why I'm spending all my time writing people up. Like any other production company, I have only a certain amount of time to process certain cases. My officers have to make

complete reports for all these other people, and it's a waste of money and time. I consider my officers to be highly professional, and they should be out there at work instead of in here writing. That's a source of aggravation to me, and it's a source of embarrassment if some of my paper is wrong. I realize it is all vital, because our statistics are taken from the reports. These statistics allow us to have so many airplanes, sedans, jeeps; they allow us to have so much gas, so much manpower, so much office space, so much staff. Without statistics we would just dry up and blow away. So it is necessary. I'm not complaining about it. I just don't think my officers should be doing work for people like the Wage Board.

HALL: If the paperwork were minimized, would that take care of all the snags?

HARRISON: There are also the courts. It is astounding the amount of knowledge officers have to have today in comparison to what it took before the courts got hold of us. Now we have to floormat everything to make the judges happy.

HALL: What do you mean "floormat"?

HARRISON: We have to have all the facts of the arrest on the report. If you stop a person on a lateral road, a road not going away from the border, you have to stop him in a certain way, and you have to be justified

Jailed woman with children, Piedras Negras, Coahuila

in stopping him. This has to be in the arrest report or the judge will throw it out just like that. If he is a documented alien who has violated his status, you've got to floormat for that. If he is an alien transported by a U.S. citizen, you've got to floormat for that. Each different case has to satisfy the justice system and the judge.

Out in California it's a lot worse than it is in Texas. They've got a lot of liberal judges out there. It's much harder to get a prosecution. And without prosecution you've got nothing, you have absolutely no deterent at

Prisoner, Piedras Negras, Coahuila

all. That's why we have such an influx of aliens. They've flooded the courts. The courts don't want to see us. The district attorney has said we're just going to take *these* cases and not those. They flat tell us that we can only prosecute the cases we can. The others we have to return voluntarily. After you do that two or three times, the aliens get pretty *bravo*. They say, "They don't do anything to me, I'll just go back over." And I don't blame them.

HALL: Then what is the answer to the alien problem?

First Communion, Highway 2, Chihuahua

HARRISON: Enforcing the law. We have good laws; we have adequate laws. But the judges won't let us enforce them. They won't let us take everyone in for prosecution. Our enforcement of the law right now amounts to us picking someone up and giving him a ride back home. If the same thing happened to you, you wouldn't be the least bit afraid of the officer.

HALL: They tell me the number of aliens being caught would be impossible to prosecute.

HARRISON: I disagree.

HALL: How would you handle it?

HARRISON: I believe we should have detention centers, adequate detention centers built along the southern border. The first offense for these people is a misdemeanor and that gets them six months in a detention facility. But I wouldn't go to that expense unless I could run it the way I wanted. I'd do it like they do at Huntsville. Those people would pay for their keep while they were in that detention center. They wouldn't earn one American dime while they were here. They would do six months' time and enough work, making concrete blocks or whatever, to pay for their existence for that six months. Then they would be sent back.

Should they repeat that offense, then it would become a felony, and they could get more time. I would give them a year in the same detention facility. I wouldn't abuse them in any way. I'd just make it necessary for them to work. I'm not advocating that we mistreat anyone in any way. I'm advocating that we detain a person who has broken the law and has no money for an adequate fine. And this would be no cost to the taxpayer. The offender would pay for his keep and pay for the facility. Those people would never come back after the first time. Or if they did and got a full year, that would end it. They could earn nothing; the profit motive would be taken out of it.

For the last twelve years we've been trying to get a bill through Congress that would punish the employer for hiring illegal aliens, but it'll probably never pass. Because people want to hire as cheap a labor as they can and sell their product for as much as they can. People who have worked illegal aliens want more of them. And they abuse them. These people are being used in prostitution and all kinds of bad things. I'm suggesting that we use the laws to protect people from that kind of treatment.

SPIRITS

1 drove into Laredo on the tail end of a tornado. Out of a black sky, gale-force winds had rolled into a funnel, dipped down into the edge of the city, and then cut right through the middle of the Confederate Air Force Airshow at the airport, leaving nearly a dozen vintage planes damaged. Trees had been ripped up or snapped in two, the streets ran like small rivers, and ankle-deep pools stood everywhere, reflecting skies that were already clearing, even though the air was still full of the strange bright smell of a vicious storm. I was reminded of what one man had once told me about the weather in this part of Texas: "We only have about fifteen inches of rainfall annually, but you sure as hell ought to be here the day we get it."

On the surface, this drowsy border town, with its tropical climate and labyrinthine streets, seems to hold few surprises. Its strong Mexican heritage is evident in everything from the flashy new downtown *mercado*, to the old plaza and the surrounding barrios like *La Ladrilla* (the brick factory), *Cantaranas* (singing frogs), *Los Amores* (the lovers), all of which could have been lifted whole from Nuevo Laredo on the other side of the river.

At La Estrella Grocery, in *La Guadalupe* barrio, Rodolfo Zamarripa sells traditional Mexican *raspas*, or snowcones, in regular flavors like strawberry and grape plus a few more challenging ones such as bubble gum, chile, cheese, and avocado, and others—*tamarindo*, nopal cactus, *guayaba*—that he says have certain medicinal properties. At Brizuela's, Eduardo or Luis Brizuela will still take measurements of your foot, make a last, and craft you a pair of boots by hand. A few doors away, at La Reynera Bakery, Jose Olguin begins at dawn rolling out *bolillos, pan dulce,* and other Mexican baked goods people here claim are equal to anything found across the bridge.

In Casa Gonzalez, Aurora Gonzalez continues the wholesale herb business her father founded almost a century ago; she buys the raw herbs

Shrine to Don Pedro Jaramillo, Laredo, Texas

Laredo, Texas

Brizuela's Boot Shop, Laredo, Texas

Owner of La Reynera Bakery, Laredo, Texas

José Olguin, baker, Laredo, Texas

from sources on both sides of the border and packages them for resale. These days, the law forbids her labeling them according to their specific traditional folk uses, but she will answer your questions about how they work. At Casa Tijerina, another of the many stores selling herbs, amulets, sprays, candles, as well as items for magic, sacred, and religious rites, one corner in front is devoted to a Don Pedrito shrine, with a life-size figure of the renowned folk healer, Don Pedro Jaramillo, surrounded by flowers and candles.

There are the poor in the barrios, but there are also the rich. In

Aurora Gonzalez and her father in Casa Gonzalez, Laredo, Texas

Yerberia,
Ojinaga,
Chihuahua

Humberto
Perez Ulloa,
Guadalupe
Bravos,
Chihuahua

Mrs. Jimmy Garza, Laredo, Texas

Laredo, Texas, I visited Mrs. Jimmy Garza in an elegant house with special handcarved furniture and a staircase custom-made in Italy and two large kitchens—one used by her cook and one reserved for her own cooking. Across the river are also the rich who live lavishly, like Laura C. de Resurdez in Nuevo Laredo, Aida T. de Trevino in Reynosa.

During any hour of the day or night, as in most other border towns, there is the incessant flow of illegals and the constant presence of the Border Patrol, combing streets, alleys, railyards, and fields in their endless vigilance. But once you slip beneath this familiar surface and are per-

*Laura C. de
Resendez,
Nuevo Laredo,
Tamaulipas*

mitted to enter certain houses, certain lives and minds, Laredo comes alive
in a different, darker way.

I was told that if anyone knew Laredo's history, both straight and
dark, it was Luciano Guajardo, head librarian for the city of Laredo. Guajardo has made a lifelong study of local folklore, which is amply reflected
in the library's collection; and he has also gained a certain reputation
about town as a ghostbuster—though he claims that "ghostbuster" is an
incorrect term, since it implies more violent and mechanical means than
he and his group employ in their efforts at coming to terms with these
supernatural beings.

Luciano Guajardo is a tall, straight man with a very strong, angular

San Xavier del Bac, Tucson, Arizona

face and a gleam in his eyes. Although he is too tall to be typical and is fair enough to be European, he has a great pride in his Mexican roots. "Ninty-nine percent of our names here are Mexican. The music and the food are Mexican; the chosen language is Spanish. In fact, I would say that at least half of our people watch Spanish language television and listen to Spanish language radio." Guajardo himself seems more comfortable speaking Spanish; in fact, when he is searching for a word in English, he always knows what it is in Spanish.

In Guajardo's view, Laredo in Texas and Nuevo Laredo in Mexico are really the same city separated by a river. But this has not always been the case. There was a time when Nuevo Laredo did not exist. For a period of three years the area between the Rio Grande and the Nueces River, which included Laredo, had been a separate country called the Republic of the Rio Grande. It was short-lived and never really gained footing, but it had a flag and a legitimate government. Then, in 1847, with the signing of the Guadalupe Hidalgo treaty between Mexico and Texas, the Rio Grande was established as the border between the two countries. "All that meant to my grandparents," said Guajardo, "was that they went to bed one night as Mexicans and awoke the next morning as Texans—without moving or being asked what they wanted."

The decision to make the Rio Grande the border did not set well with everyone. "One hundred and thirty-five families got together and held a public meeting," Guajardo explained. "They did not denounce the Republic of Texas, but they did declare their love for Mexico. They decided they would cross the river and live over there. They gathered their belongings, they dismantled their houses and they unburied their dead. Yes, their dead," he repeated. "They wanted the remains of their ancestors on Mexican soil. That settlement became Nuevo Laredo. And as far as I know, it is the only town in the world that was settled for patriotic reasons alone."

No matter where the official border lies, Laredo is still more closely tied to Mexico in spirit than to the United States. Included are the black arts and a preoccupation with religion that thrive in Mexico. Someone revealed that Laredo has 259 card readers. There are numerous other kinds of *curanderos* and healers, as well. The world-famous Silva Self Mind Control Center was born here. The town seems to be full of believers and practicioners of folk medicine and parapsychology. "I think," said Guajardo, very much aware of these phenomena, "this is more prevalent in the world than we know. Here, because of our heritage, we are less embarrassed to admit these things than other people are." He smiled and rummaged through a file for a lecture he had once given on *curanderos*, healers.

"However," he said, cocking his head characteristically, "I would venture to say from my experience—and, mind you, all I have to go by is what is in my head—that 80 or 90 percent of all those Sister Annas and Sister Patricias, all those people who claim to help you in any which way, are fakes. Just yesterday I heard a radio ad for a man in Rio Grande City. The list of things the man could do was staggering. It's understandable, because there's a lot of money in it. Still, I say most of them are charlatans."

He had an example as fresh as the previous week. "A family that I know had a brother in the hospital with symptoms of a stroke. The doctors said it was not a stroke, but they could not tell what it was. He was there for a month. They came to me and asked if I thought they should go see someone across the river—somebody had recommended a woman. I had never heard of her. They asked me to go with them, and I said all right.

"This woman had a huge waiting room. You had to pick a number and wait until she would see you. Finally, we went into her consulting room. It was a sight. Oh God, more things hanging on the walls—devils, saints, crosses of all kinds, unusual little things—the normal stuff for these people.

"The *curandera* was putting on her make-up," Guajardo declared with a grimace. "My friends told her all about their brother. His wife had died six months ago. He had been very dedicated to her. He never drank, he never smoked, he never ran around. Now he'd been in the hospital a month, and the doctors could find nothing to explain his condition."

*Luciano
Guajardo,
Laredo, Texas*

Guajardo leaned forward in his chair, almost in imitation of the woman peering into her little mirror, daubing at her face. "This *curandera* sits for a minute, still putting on her eye shadow. She stopped. And her diagnosis, if you could call it that, was this: 'Well, I must tell you that somebody has put a hex on your brother—somebody who loved him very much as a young man. The only thing that makes it hard is that the woman who loved him is dead now. It is going to be a little harder to cure him. But I'll tell you what, you bring me two thousand six hundred dollars, and I am sure I can make him well.'

"The two sisters looked at each other dumbfounded. They didn't have that kind of money. The *curandera* had gone back to putting on her make-up. After all, she said, two thousand six hundred dollars isn't very much to save a life. I am sure you can borrow the money and repay it."

Without qualification, Guajardo placed that woman in the 80 to 90 percent he called charlatans and fakes. One giveaway was her charging a fixed sum. He maintained that the real *curanderos* made no such charges. They needed money to live, of course; but people gave them money

Curandera's table, Laredo, Texas

Near Tijuana

according to what they could afford or what they felt like paying. Of that other 10 to 20 percent, the ones he did not consider to be fakes, he said simply, "I am sure they have certain powers."

I asked if I could meet one. Yes, he said. He knew of two mental healers, two very good ones. One was Pancho Montemayor in Nuevo Laredo; the other was Raul Villaverde in Laredo. He knew Pancho was away in San Antonio, but he thought I should be able to see Raul Villaverde.

Gisela Valdez, a friend who'd kindly shown me the area, helped me find the mobile home on Callaghan Street where Villaverde lived with his daughter and her husband. Inside, Villaverde adjusted a blue and white

floor fan so the cool air would include us as it swung back and forth. He sat in a rocking chair in front of a wall filled with an impressive collection of classical music albums and tapes. To my right, in the small kitchenette, Villaverde's daughter was frying meat and heating chili for her husband's lunch. The smell of it came in waves, pushed back as the fan came my way and flowing in as it swung toward Villaverde.

Nothing about Raul Villaverde came even close to the classic picture of a mental healer one might conjure up. There was no hocus-pocus, no magical trappings or paraphernalia, no weird garb. He wore shorts and running shoes and a large gold amulet of Christ. About the only unusual thing were his eyes. They shone clear and very intense, almost piercing.

Villaverde calls his power a gift and claims he discovered it while he was taking a Silva Mind Control course in the mid 1950s. "It was a long time ago," he said, "but I think I was in his sixth group." As he learned more about the Silva principles, he found he had a special power; he tested it out on himself, curing an allergy from which he had suffered for years.

Since then he has treated many people. He maintains frankly that there are limits to what he is able to do. He cannot, for example, cure a person with cancer that has spread through their body, though he can greatly lessen their pain and suffering. Cancer that is curable is a different matter; he has cured malignant tumors, shrinking them appreciably each time he "sees" the patient.

He doesn't need to know or even meet the person he is going to treat, but he must know the person's name and age. They can be miles away and unaware that he has been asked to treat them. And he believes that subconsciously they do know, that they are seeking help, and that either their mind comes to him or they allow his mind to go to them.

His method is simple. He shuts his eyes and works while his mind is at the alpha level, something that is taught in the Silva course. It is at this point that his vision is clearest. He snaps his fingers to get his mind there and then snaps them again and again, at odd intervals, to keep himself at the alpha level. "It is like sound waves," he told me, "like radio waves. I make contact with the person I am seeing in my mind. I can see the sickness in them. It is like little flashing lights or, in the case of an organ, it glows red, purple, yellow. Once I have located the problem, I can operate and inject—if those measures are necessary."

I asked what he felt had been his most difficult cure.

His reply came fast: leukemia. He had cured two cases. One was a young Mexican boy nine years old. He had received a telephone call from the boy's uncle, explaining the situation, asking for help. He visualized the boy and began talking to him, working with him. As he worked, his method came to him. He put a tube in the boy's body, in the area of his kidneys, to drain out the diseased blood. Then, above the boy's shoulders, he put a vessel containing clean blood and plasma. He inserted a tube into the boy's neck so the good blood could run into his body while the bad blood drained out. He repeated the treatment on this child he had neither met nor seen for the next eight or nine days. At the end of that time, the boy went to a hospital in Monterrey, Mexico, for tests. The doctors were astounded. The leukemia was gone from his body.

There was a silence, dulled only by the hum of the fan and the rustle of paper as the breeze swept over a magazine on the floor. Raul relaxed; he clasped his right hand around his left. Then he turned and looked directly at Gisela.

She spoke almost automatically. She told him that her youngest child had asthma, that he loved sports, but as soon as he got in the grass he began developing allergies. Very often she had to rush him to the hospital.

"What is his name?" Raul asked.

She told him.

"What is his age?"

She told him.

Raul closed his eyes. He sat up straighter in the rocking chair. He snapped his fingers. His head moved slightly, as if finding the right spot. He snapped his fingers again. After a moment, he reached out with his hands. It seemed he brought a body before him and began examining it.

"He's small for his age—very slender—"

"Yes—" said Gisela hesitantly.

He continued to "look" at the child with his fingers. "He has brown hair."

"Yes."

"Brown eyes, shaped like yours."

"Yes."

I could feel Gisela becoming uneasy. *Curanderos, brujas,* card readers, herbalists were a part of her culture that, like many other middle-class Mexican-Americans, she felt her higher education had helped her shed and leave behind. "I keep telling him he's getting better," she spoke up, as if to reassure herself. "And I think he is. I haven't had to take him to the hospital once this year." There was an edge of fright in her voice.

Villaverde snapped his fingers, maintaining his trance, staying at the alpha level, working. His fingers traced their way along the child's spine, counting down the vertebrae; it seemed he took something away and put it over his shoulder. He turned the body. It looked as if his fingers had found the boy's lungs. "Otherwise, his lungs are usually clear."

"Yes—"

The fingers climbed higher, to the face. "But there is trouble with the sinuses."

Now she only nodded.

Villaverde's efforts became more intense. It seemed he was trying to move himself into the child's body, to teach the boy to heal himself. His face contorted. He breathed in, held his breath, forced it into his mouth until his lips pursed out. He released it. He repeated the process.

Finally, he stopped. His shoulders dropped slowly, relaxing, and he sat completely motionless. He opened his eyes and sat there blinking. He let his back relax against the chair. After a few seconds, he spoke. "Your son will be finished with his allergies in fifteen days."

He had, he said, injected him. As further treatment he prescribed a glass of water each night for the fifteen days (this was, I recalled, the treatment most often prescribed by Don Pedro Jaramillo, the great healer who'd come out of Mexico to practice in the border country). The boy was to drink the first half of the glass before going to sleep—to help him sleep soundly, "to give him good dreams." The other half he was to drink in the morning when he woke up. And he was to tell himself that it would make him well, for in it would be the medicine. Mentally, Villaverde made his rounds each night, adding what was needed to the waiting glasses of water.

I met Gisela's child for the first time that evening. The moment I saw him I felt I had seen him before—so accurate had Villaverde's description been. And the child himself spoke of a strange feeling he'd had that day, a queasiness that had come over him at school. Gisela asked what time it was. She hadn't needed to, of course; I knew it would have been the time we were at Raul Villaverde's.

On another morning, back in the stacks of the public library, where Luciano Guajardo seemed most comfortable, he spoke of the force that had opened the threshold of his belief. "My mother," he said, "was an illiterate person. She couldn't even read Spanish and, of course, she read no English. She was very superstitious. She believed there was an evil force and she believed in the supernatural. She also believed in God, mind you—God and the Virgin of Guadalupe and that whole army of saints. Nobody dared say anything, even jokingly, about one of those saints." He wagged his finger and laughed.

"We didn't go to church every Sunday. We didn't go to confession every first Friday of the month. She was not that much of a fanatic Catholic. But don't you dare say 'God' or 'Goddamit,' because then there was trouble.

"My mother was afraid of ghosts, and she was afraid of witches. We grew up with threats of exorcism. Everytime we behaved beyond the endurance of our parents, she would say, 'I'm going to take you to St. Augustin and have the priest take the devil out of you.' She never used the word 'exorcism,' *exorcismo*, she just said *Hay que te sacar el diablo.* We thought that would be very painful. I don't know why, but we were afraid.

"She thought that a storm was God's punishment on us. There was a ritual she went through with each storm. At the first sound of thunder or the first sight of lightning, even at a distance, we were all gathered in and made to stay in the house. We could not stand near a door or a window. She would cover all the mirrors and she would cover our heads—with something, even a handkerchief or a napkin—because she claimed hair attracted electricity. She could prove it with a comb and a piece of paper. Well, we were children, and we went along with it.

"To make it worse was her insistence that the family go through the storms in almost complete darkness. To avoid attracting lightning, she would cut the main power switch. We would go through the storm with only the light of one or two little sacred candles. And these candles had been stolen from the altar of St. Augustin. They used to sell those little long candles to burn at the altar, and, as soon as they were small, the caretaker would take them out to throw away. But he would sell them to my mother and others like her. These were very, very sacred, and they were lit whenever there was a big storm.

"Then, with all this ritual finished, she would take the youngest child in the family and have him or her cut the storm in two. She would do this by opening the back door to the kitchen, putting a knife in the child's hands and then, guiding the child's hands with hers, she would make the sign of the cross, to cut the storm in half, while she prayed." Guajardo makes the appropriate gesture in the air. "I remembered that many times—I would almost say all of the time, except maybe memory fails me—the storm would subside after it had been cut in half."

The depth of her faith was amazing, even to Guajardo, whose own preoccupations with the supernatural run to relatively uncommon lengths. "One of her treasures was a footprint traced on that old fine tissue paper they used to sell. In Spanish, it's called *papel de chine*. It was even finer than what we call onion skin. It was a little piece of paper on which someone had outlined this footprint. And she claimed that whoever gave it to her or whomever she bought it from swore it was the footprint of the Virgin Mary." He raised both hands to signify, almost with relief, that it was her statement, not his. "Not that the Virgin Mary had put her foot there. No, it was traced from another, from another, from another, in a line reaching back in time; and my mother believed it came from a tracing of the original outline of the Virgin's footprint."

His voice grew softer. "The footprint was my mother's treasure. Hardly anyone saw it. And she wouldn't let anyone take a tracing from her copy. Occasionally—I know of at least three or four times, and this was a dilemma for mother because these were very good *comadres* or very dear distant relatives to whom she could not easily say no—someone asked her for it. Usually, she said no—No, I'm sorry, but it loses its force, it loses its charm if it is traced. But there were at least three or four people she could not say no to. However, in tracing it she would deviate a little bit from the original footprint on her paper. She would make the arch a little bigger or a little smaller. She would do something so no one had it exactly as she had it."

The phone rang; Guajardo's line buzzed. He took the call in Spanish and then asked that we not be disturbed. "It used to be that there were people who gathered all sorts of *oraciónes*, all sorts of prayers. Mother was one of these. There are common prayers that everyone knows, but there are also prayers for other things, strange things." Naturally, those were the prayers she collected and kept to be lent.

"There was a prayer called *La oración para ayudar a buen morir*, a prayer that would help you to a more peaceful death. People in the neighborhood came sometimes to borrow it from my mother or to ask her to go out and recite it. Mother didn't read it; she knew it by heart. It was a prayer to help a hopeless person go sooner and not be a burden on the poor family. For that prayer she used a very special crucifix—special and rare. The cross had a Christ on it, and his feet were nailed to the cross, but the right foot was over the left foot. I noticed from then on that every other cross I've seen had the feet the other way around. So maybe there was something to it."

As a young man, Luciano Guajardo developed his interest in ghosts by reading everything about them that he could get his hands on. After years of study, that initial interest had become belief. "I believe," he said with conviction, "what I have seen. I am not a Doubting Thomas. Just because you see it and I don't doesn't mean anything to me. Maybe you were privileged to see it and I wasn't. But I didn't just wake up one day believing in it. It came through the years. I delved into just about everything that had anything to do with the supernatural—card readings of both ordinary playing cards and tarot cards, tea-leaf readings, séances—everything."

His belief in ghosts grew with his knowledge of them and their habits. He studied the subject for years before it ever occurred to him that he might do something concrete about it, that he might actually see or communicate with a supernatural being. And that came as the eventual result of a discussion in a small restaurant. He was part of a group of local businessmen and professionals who often met there late at night after various meetings to have coffee and talk, to wind down before going home.

"One night," he recalled, "the subject of ghosts came up. Right away, there were a few of us interested. And it turned out that every one of us, because of some childhood experience or something that had happened to a parent of grandparent, had a belief in ghosts. We decided to continue talking about it. A week or two later the conversation continued. Four more people joined the table. It grew until there were at least fourteen of us.

"Among that number are doctors and lawyers, people whose professions would be hurt if they were to admit it publically. So we formed a secret society—not that we were doing anything clandestine; it was only to protect the ones who would suffer from public disclosure. Our interest grew to the point where we began seriously to look into some of the things that came our way. I don't want to sound like a doctor, but now we get more cases than we can handle."

Because they were for the most part professional men, they approached the business of ghosts with seriousness. "We like to think we do a very thorough job on those cases we decide to follow," Guajardo assured me. "We have investigated some things that go so far back that there are no records available. It's not like picking up a telephone and dialing to see who you make contact with."

Kino Church,
Sonora

Highway 2,
Sonora

West of
Presidio, Texas

One of their most successful cases concerned an old woman in black. At one time she had owned a sizeable piece of property in downtown Laredo, and it was there she had returned to haunt. There had been a big house, a carriage house, stables, and other buildings. For over fifty years they had been occupied by a Catholic school run by nuns of the Salesian Order. Then the nuns built their own school and moved out. A number of the buildings were used as storage. But one building, which had been the gymnasium, the carriage house in the original scheme of things, was rented and converted to a used clothing store.

"After five or six months," Guajardo stated, "the salesgirls began to notice some strange things. They were never really bothered until one day one of them saw a lady dressed in black come in. They didn't notice until later that she never carried a purse. One girl asked if she could help her. The woman said she'd go back to the corner where they kept the overcoats. It was close to closing time and the girl in charge started putting out the lights. The clerk said there was a woman back in overcoats. They went back there but they didn't find her. No one thought much of it; she had probably gone out unnoticed.

"Two weeks later a woman in black came in just before closing. She told the clerk she wanted to use the bathroom. Which was not unusual. Again, it came time to close, and the clerk said there was a woman in the bathroom. But when they checked, no one was there."

It happened a third time, a fourth, a fifth. The salesgirls tried to compare notes about the woman; but no one could remember more than her black clothing and something else they could never quite put into words. Sometimes they would find her inside and no one could remember seeing her come in. The girls began being more afraid of her.

"The cashier, who incidentally was the same cashier who used to work at the restaurant where we started hanging out," explained Guajardo, "began to talk about it to the group. He asked if we could do something. Yes, I said, but we needed permission from the owner of the store and the owners of the property. We secured those permissions. They said we could do anything as long as we didn't destroy any part of the house."

Guajardo was more animated now. He was into the kind of detail he enjoyed—the search, the research, the supporting facts that took it all out of the realm of pure speculation. "We checked the abstract. The property is one block west of what was once the city cemetery, the records of which are no longer available. The land had been in the same family since the original Spanish land grant. We couldn't find any strange deaths, suicides, murders, or anything else that was suspicious. However, we did find that the last people to live in the house were very odd—an old lady and a young man, her son."

On the surface, that in itself did not seem serious. But as they engaged in more investigating and dug up more information, the strange activities at the used clothing store increased. Things were being moved; articles were misplaced. Which only intensified the interest of the group. It was decided they would definitely try to make contact and figure out what the "someone" or "something" wanted.

Guajardo described the man his group had used as a medium to contact the spirit of the woman. "Through the years," Guajardo said, "we have found a person who is very unique. He is a destitute, always begging someone for coffee. He is funny looking, but he is not ugly. He is an enigma to those of us who know him because the man talks and talks and talks and talks and talks. And you can never make sense of what he is talking about unless you know the subject. He will change subjects at the drop of a syllable. He can be talking about medicine, and if you are a doctor you know he knows what he is talking about—though he has had no training in the subject. Then at the wink of an eye, without telling you why or reaching any conclusion, he'll change the subject and begin talking about something totally different."

He paused to shrug his shoulders and smile. "We are sure, without any scientific testing, that this man is probably devoid of a soul. And all of these things that he says that are above your head and above mine just all of a sudden go into him and he says them—so they will go out.

"Three times we have used him to make contact with a ghost. The first time, I would say, he didn't stop talking long enough for the ghost to speak to him. The second time he was able to give us some detail about the encounter. And we got him to agree to look at this thing in the used clothing store."

The man was reluctant. Guajardo and his associates persisted and finally he said he would try it. He chose a Thursday night. He said they should lock him inside at six o'clock, as soon as the store closed for the night. They were to shut off the lights and lock him in; but they were to wait just outside the door, ready to open it immediately when he called out.

"We locked him in. It didn't start right away. We kept hoping. We heard one noise, and then we heard another one. And we heard him yell out to her: IS THAT YOU, DOÑA ISABEL?"

They overheard through the thick doors a curious one-way conversation, half of which they could only guess.

"It was like someone talking on the telephone," said Guajardo. "We heard him arguing with somebody. We heard him try to interrupt somebody who was talking. He said he was there to find out who she was, what she wanted, what we could do to help her. She would obviously go on talking because he kept trying to interrupt her by saying: 'It's not what you think. I keep telling you they're not here for that.'

"About forty-five minutes later, after this long conversation, there was a knock on the door. We opened it and out came the man. He sat down on the steps, as if he was worn out. 'Finally,' he said, 'I have talked to her. It is all settled.' We kept asking: What happened? What is it? But he sat there, as if dazed."

They pestered the contact until he talked. He told them, first, how

Nuevo Laredo,
Tamaulipas

El Paso, Texas

elusive she had been to reach—even once she was in the room. She didn't want to talk. "Finally," Guajardo said, sighing as though he were going through it all again, "after a few minutes of talking to whatever was there, he said Doña Isabel was a very wealthy widow and she had an only son. She had always had a fear of dying alone. Consequently, she didn't want the son to marry and leave her. She told the contact she had always persuaded the girls who came to the house with the interest of marrying him to keep away from him—this was during their lifetime. And she tried to convince the son that they were gold diggers or that they were too fat or too ugly. And the man, being very much attached to the mother, believed her."

According to Guajardo's analysis, there had been no problem, no real threat to the mother, during the long period the property was occupied by the nuns. However, when the school moved, and the used clothing store had opened up with three women working there, Doña Isabel's old fears had been awakened.

"Yes, there are women," the contact had argued, and, "yes, one of them is no longer married. But they are not here to marry your son. They have their own families. Even the girl without a husband has two children to support. They are here to work."

As Guajardo put it, the woman had not seemed very convinced, but she stopped bothering the girls in the used clothing store. In fact, there was not another incident until the devaluation of the peso broke the border economy and forced the owner of the store to close its doors.

"After the clothing store moved," Guajardo said, his voice falling a note, "the school district took over the whole complex. To this day, with all these new young female teachers, Doña Isabel occasionally comes out. She tries to frighten them away. If they work at night, she turns the lights out. She flings boxes of pencils on the floor. I understand that one day she even disturbed every desk in there, moving the contents from one desk to another until no desk was the same as it had been."

Had they gone back and taken the contact for another session?

Guajardo shook his head sadly. "No. We aren't allowed to go in there now. The schools don't want to do anything about it. They'd be too embarrassed to admit it."

That, too, was Laredo—the difference between official Laredo and private Laredo. And the situation would have been the same in Mexico.

There were other stories, old stories he had only heard about and still others about cases he had helped solve. He looked at it all as a scientist would, trying to back up each episode with solid fact. Things had a purpose, a cause, an effect, even fantastic things. There was a logic to what he was doing about ghosts, a logic in the way he was approaching it. And he had been fortunate enough by being born there on the border to have access to two worlds, the fanciful world of Mexico and the pragmatic world of the United States. He had brought them together in a way different from any I had seen. The combination allowed him license to travel these strange territories. And I had the feeling that although he might not readily admit it, Luciano Guajardo felt that, like Raul Villaverde, he, too, had been chosen to do a work that was only just now finding its time.

RANCHERS

People ordinarily think of the border in terms of towns; indeed, "bordertown" has become a figure of speech, a word in the language. But most of the border is land, ranches and farms that people have grazed or kept under cultivation for centuries and some stretches of land too desolate and inhospitable to support any life beyond cactus and the kind of brush no animal chooses to eat. It runs from tropical to arid, from rich, fertile soil capable of producing three or four crops a year to raw wilderness whose only purpose seems to be to record the slow eroding grind of time and seasons.

Ralph Johnson knows this land. He reaches down with his large, incredibly calloused hand and feels the dirt the way a designer might feel a width of silk. He is a big man whose faded "501" jeans and chambray shirt were never stonewashed to be worn as mere decoration. He was born on the border. His father moved from Texas into this part of New Mexico, known mostly for the 1916 raid Pancho Villa made on Columbus, the town that lies a few miles to the east on State Highway 9. Ralph still runs the ranch his father bought, which has its southern fence line right on the border. He has been here all his life—except for the time he spent away fighting the Second World War.

"When I came out of the Navy," he told me, "what we had here was strictly a cow ranch. That was after the Depression and the war, and, needless to say, it was in pretty decrepit condition. We considered that if we dug a well here and recovered seven gallons of water a minute we were lucky as hell."

Trusting luck, however, was no way to deal with the demands made by the advances of modern agriculture, with its accelerated production schedules and narrow profit margins. They had to adapt or go under. At first, they were growing only feed for their cattle and cotton. Those crops couldn't yield the kind of income the ranch needed to grow and compete.

Man in Ejido
Ortiz de
Dominguez

***Ralph Johnson
and sons,
Columbus,
New Mexico***

"With the high cost of energy and machinery and everything, we had to change to higher-risk, higher-profit crops—tomatoes, onions, chile—"

That change of planting schedule, coupled with Ralph's determination, had set the Johnson place apart from most of the nearby farms and ranches, some of which were struggling to stay solvent, while others were already abandoned or up for auction. "We do have a pretty diversified place," he admitted. He was sitting in his office, which was that day being outfitted with a new multiline phone system, another efficiency measure to save time and fuel. "We have a cattle ranch. We have a gin and an onion shed. We own our own farm. We farm cheaper than most people, because we can buy everything wholesale."

By whatever means they had done it, the Johnson place stood out. As I had driven along Highway 9 through dry, buckskin-colored hills dotted with the tall plumelike blossoms of the yucca, the neatly cultivated green stretches of the Johnson farms, with Mexico smoldering in the background, had come as a jarring surprise. Seen with the sophisticated machinery, large outbuildings, and modern bungalows belonging to Johnson and his son (the younger boy lived a few miles farther west, in the old ranch

Chickens in Coahuila

Red chile harvest near Redford, Texas

house), it was testament both to the ingenuity and expertise of these men and to their desire to make the place pay.

I asked Ralph what kept him fighting the odds of life on the border, why he hadn't moved to an area where the work was easier.

"Well, I might just not know any better," he said, in a moment of dry humor that made his two sons grin. He went on, seriously, to list his preferences, his values: "I like it here. To me, it's the most productive area of the country—and I've been all over the country. I've always lived here and always been able to make a living. It's a good place to have a family, to

Cotton pickers, Highway 2, near El Porvenir, Chihuahua

bring up kids. It's home to us. We're gonna stay here through good, bad, and indifferent. Hell, I doubt if I could sell out anyway. No, it's not for sale. Never has been. We'll be here from now on—unless we go broke."

I asked if he used any labor out of Mexico.

He seemed a little weary of the question, or maybe it was only the idea that made him sigh.

"Yeah, we work wetbacks," he declared. It was something they did more out of necessity than actual preference. "We'd sooner not have them—because of the Border Patrol and the fact that our kind of farming is a twenty-four-hour job. But any wetback that works here draws at least minimum wage, some of them draw far better. I'll put it this way, if there would be a local that would take the job, we'd far rather have him. Like here at the gin or the onion shed, we try to stay with locals as much as we possibly can."

The Johnsons had the same problems with local workers that I'd heard echoed by employers everywhere along the border; the relative ease and comfort of Welfare had made workers reluctant to take the hard jobs. "This far out in the tulies and this being hard work and hot work, you don't always get locals. I know some people don't believe this, but we try to hire as many locals as we can get."

Aside from the wets they employed, Ralph had his own hard-line policy about Mexicans. "We just don't let them come over here," he stated firmly. "That way there's no problem with theft. We don't even let the ones just passing through go through. We call the Border Patrol or run them back to the fence. With the ranch land, we can't hold them back."

He pointed to the south, where I could make out the buildings of a small Mexican settlement sparkling in the sun. "See that *ejido* there— there's another one five miles over the hill. The people that live in them places, they don't have a damn thing to do but watch us. If we're gone, here they come. That's what we're up against. It's plain as day to us. There's that little town, with no visible means of support, so there's got to be something. They've got to be running dope or stealing something, because there's no other way they can make a living."

Ralph had a story. It showed exactly what could happen if they let down their twenty-four-hour vigilance. "Several years ago we was cutting corn on the west farm and we'd been patrolling it every night. We hadn't lost a bit. One night we went into this little fair they have up in Deming. (We always buy a sheep or calf or something to help the 4-H and FFA out.) We shut the combines down at five o'clock and went to town. We left the lights working and everything just like we was here. The boys stayed to the dance, and I came home at about eleven o'clock. I told my wife I was going to whip through these farms, make sure everything was all right. I didn't see nothing. But the next morning I was watching the combines. They'd go ten feet and stop, ten feet and stop. I wondered what the hell was going on. I walked into the corn and here were these damn sacks of corn, all sacked up and sewn shut. The only night we'd been gone—and then it was only about six hours, these Mexicans out of that *ejido* had come in there and started stripping the ears off the stalks and hauling them away. That's what we're up against. They don't have a damn thing to do but watch us."

For probably the same reason, they have trouble keeping the border fences mended. It has been a constant job, requiring an ongoing expenditure of money and time. Recently, too, they contracted with the State of New Mexico to put in five miles of new fence along the border between their place and Columbus. "We put it up, and it was a hell of a fence—

Woman in ejido,
Sonora

Man in ejido,
Sonora

Paula Vega,
ejido in
Chihuahua

Kitchen in
Ejido del
Desierto,
Sonora

steel posts set in concrete, steel braces, six strands of wire. We finished it, and the governor, Toney Anaya, and the press and a bunch of others came down here to inspect it. So we all drove down to the easiest place to look at the fence, and there before us, as big as life, was a gaping damn hole. It had been cut the night before, and you could still see the car tracks."

It was an embarrassment, but it was also a border reality. On the day we spoke, Ralph said he thought that five miles of fence were cut in at least four or five places. Smugglers did it, to crash across with contraband. Or the farmers did it to drive their cattle through to feed on the failed and abandoned farms.

Family in Ejido Ortiz de Dominguez

He stopped talking and picked up a short length of white wire the telephone installer had left on the desk. He tied a knot in the wire and pulled it tight. "You may get from this interview that I don't think too much of Mexico," he said, pausing. "You're right. I've lived here too long. The farthest I've been into that country is horseback—just the other side of Palomas—and that's as far as I'm ever going to go."

He was adamant. "We've always had trouble with the Mexicans. The first I can remember was with a thousand head of cattle dad drove over into Mexico. The government was going to confiscate them. They put soldiers around the herd and told this foreman with the herd they wanted ten thousand dollars' ransom. The foreman wired dad and asked what he should do. Dad said to bring them across at any cost. So they brought them out under gunfire."

It isn't so much the Mexicans as the country. "When I was a kid I went to school in a little old one-room schoolhouse. There was me and usually seven little Mexicans. That's because it took eight kids to keep a school open. If there wasn't eight, Dad just went and hired another Mexican so there'd be enough kids to keep the school open. They always had plenty of kids. So all my life I've grown up with them. Mexicans are okay. But to my way of thinking, that's not a free country at all. It's just as different across that fence over there as night and day. The average Mexican doesn't have any freedom whatsoever. Two years ago, they told them that if they didn't vote—even though there's only one party—they couldn't register their cars. Right now, the only way out is to come over here."

Weeks later, I slipped onto the plaza in Ojinaga, Chihuahua, to catch the pink glow of the early morning light on the church. It was a large, barren square that probably didn't have a best season. A man walked down the steps of the church toward me. I thought he wanted money. But we only exchanged greetings. He said it was good to hear gringos talking a little Spanish, then he asked where I was from. He told me he knew the United States. He'd had to work in many different states, on places like the Ralph Johnson Farms, to keep his family alive. He mentioned Texas, Oklahoma, New Mexico, Colorado, Kansas. "There's no money here," he said. He maintained that Mexico could have the same kind of farms; it could support the people who went away. There was the same kind of fertile soil, the same opportunities. But there was a serious stumbling block to such progress: the politics of Mexico. "It's that goddamn sonofabitch of a president, De la Madrid." (All of his profanity was in English.) "People are hungry, they're cold, they're dying. Everybody's poor here."

A few hundred miles farther along the border, Leticia Lewis, a Mexican woman married to an American, said a solution was simple: "Mexico needs a miracle."

Her own "miracle" was that she lived in Eagle Pass, Texas, where everything worked. And, of course, she wasn't poor. "I think I have the best of both worlds," she said. "I have the United States, and I have Mexico. For example, last Sunday evening I came home from Mexico and

Ojinaga, Chihuahua

Near Eagle Pass, Texas

my lights were flickering. I called the emergency number for the electric company. It was eleven o'clock at night but they came right over and had the transformer fixed in no time. In Mexico that would have taken two or three weeks. It is amazing. In Mexico, we have a saying—*After God, the gringos.*"

Her husband, Peter, spent the major part of every week on their ranch in Mexico. Sometimes Leticia visited him (she called these "conjugal visits"); but most of the time Peter drove back to Eagle Pass for weekends. They didn't really consider the drive across the river leaving Mexico. To them, Eagle Pass was a part of the U.S. in name only. Another local resident had put it this way: "I just don't believe the United States ever starts until you get past Uvalde"—a town about sixty-five miles to the north.

The language had something to do with it. "The only people I speak English to around here are my parents," Peter said. "Every place else you speak Spanish—at the cleaners, at the grocery."

Peter, too, felt the strain of their separation, but he preferred living in the country. I asked if it was the challenge of working the ranch or the isolation. He pondered that idea a moment then decided it was both. But he understood why Leticia wanted to stay in Eagle Pass, an acceptance of

Lucio family,
Coahuila

facts that probably allowed their marriage to continue to work. "Mexicans are an urban people. They're not like Americans, who like to go off and live in the country by themselves. That kind of life is very unusual for Mexicans because by nature they are very gregarious."

Leticia felt there was another difference, one that went deeper and explained a great deal about problems in understanding between the two countries: "We Mexicans have a good sense of humor. We don't cry very much over crises or catastrophies. We make a joke or sing a song. You Anglos go out and gather statistics and write down all kinds of numbers. We always come out with a song or a new joke."

I had been places where the sense of humor might have been there, but it was overwhelmed by the seriousness of the economic crisis that was dragging more and more Mexicans deeper into poverty. Inside a small store in an *ejido* the week before, I had watched while a Mexican man brought in a large burlap bag full of shelled corn and put it on the scales.

The woman tending the store said it was worth one hundred pesos (at that time approximately twenty cents, U.S.). Understandably, he looked dejected. That sack of corn represented hours of work.

Alberto Muzquiz has used the border as a vital element in his cattle business for a number of years. His hometown is Muzquiz in the state of Coahuila. The name of the town was changed to Muzquiz from Presidio de Santa Rosa de Lima after his great-great-uncle, who in the last century served as an interim president of Mexico. Alberto's wife, Cornelia, was also born in Mexico, but of American parents, which meant she held dual citizenship until the age of eighteen, when she chose to be a U.S. citizen. Now they move back and forth between La Rosita, their ranch in Mexico, and their home in Eagle Pass, Texas.

Like Ralph Johnson, Alberto is an intelligent, enterprising rancher using his ingenuity to try and make ranching pay. "I follow my product,

Rosa Isela Muñoz de Ramirez and Luis Ramirez Olivares, U.S. side of Rio Grande, near El Paso, Texas

which is cattle, across the border," Alberto said on a September morning in Eagle Pass. We were having a breakfast of spicy menudo in the Copper Kettle Restaurant and waiting for the sky to clear enough so we could fly to his ranch in Mexico. "In my case," he said, "I can follow them. I lease some country over here in the United States and try to stretch them out a little bit so I can make a little money. Some people call it vertical integration. Mine is not that in the truest sense. I raise the calves at home and then grow them out over here in Texas. Sometimes I even take them all the way to the feedlot, waiting for the price to get right. In fact, the only thing I haven't done is butcher them and peddle the meat myself."

He smiled and measured more chopped raw onion, bits of fiery jala-

Cowboy, Coahuila

peño, and oregano into the bowl of cooked tripe and mixed it with a spoon. "Let me show you what I mean." He drew a credit-card calculator out of his vest pocket and sped through a mind-boggling series of figures to show how it was possible to make it work. In all the days I was with Alberto, in Mexico and the United States, he was always reaching for the calculator or a pencil to demonstrate this point or prove that point.

"That's the idea," he said, putting the calculator away. "I try to work both sides of the river to stretch my income a little bit by generating a few dollars over here. Sometimes it works, sometimes it doesn't. I bring my calves from the other side of the border, and that's the end of that operation. The profit, if any, goes to the Mexico ranch. I start a whole new business here, a different ball game. In other words, if I lose money on my steers over here, I don't charge the losses to my Mexico operation. I've got a bunch I'm thinking of putting in the feedlot now—to prolong the agony," he laughed.

I had understood that it was difficult to bring animals out of Mexico.

"People have been exporting cattle to the United States since before the turn of the century. They kept it up until the fifties, when there was an outbreak of hoof-and-mouth disease. They closed the border until it was wiped out."

Gradually, the morning fog rose up and blew off the river, and there was enough visibility to fly. We crossed the highway to the small Eagle Pass airport. Alberto continued to talk about bringing cattle into the U.S. It was difficult, but I think it presented challenges he actually enjoyed. The cattle could be brought only from the northern states of Mexico. A line across the interior had been established years ago. And there were certain complicated steps you had to take. They had to be disease-free and free of fever ticks, which had been wiped out in Texas in the twenties but which still existed in Mexico. In order to insure that there were no fever ticks, they had to be dipped (swum through a bath) twice within a fifteen-day period. Then they were brought to the border for inspection. That meant each animal had to be individually checked by inspectors and veterinarians before it would be allowed onto a truck to the United States. If one tick was found on one steer then the whole herd was refused.

One afternoon, while I was having coffee with Peter, I overheard a phone conversation from Piedras Negras in which he learned that the inspectors had found a tick in his load of steers. They would have to be dipped again, kept in the pens, fed for ten days, and then tested a second time. That expense would take much of the profit away from the shipment.

Together, Alberto and I pushed open the long sliding door on the front of his hangar. "There's one regulation after another," he continued. "The paperwork is incredible. The joke among most ranchers is that it takes one truck to haul the livestock and two more to haul the various papers and permits required to get them moved."

I laughed.

"It's not as exaggerated as it sounds," he said, opening the cowl on the engine and reaching in for the dipstick. "There are three government departments in Mexico City that have to approve applications for the exportation of cattle."

After Alberto got his Cessna in the air and the throttle was cut, reducing the engine noise, we could talk again. He circled over Eagle Pass. He said he had bought the house in Eagle Pass because of his three kids. "They're being educated in the States. We still consider Mexico our home. But this is where the kids are going to school."

All of it fit some kind of master plan Alberto had worked out—the

Alberto
Muzquiz

school, the ranch in Mexico, crossing the Mexican steers, land leased in Texas. I could almost see him at his calculator. It had not been without its ups and downs. "As of 1982, life on the border has been one crisis after another. Just when you think it's getting kind of stabilized, all of a sudden there is another peso scare or something."

I liked Alberto enormously. He was a big man who wore scuffed high-heeled boots and a wide hat, and he carried himself with great style. He was almost always smiling, ready with the jokes that Leticia had said were typical of Mexicans, though he was just as quick with his little calculator, with the figures and numbers. He seemed to know everyone. People stopped him on the street, on the highway, in restaurants, everywhere, to shake hands. He had a great respect for the United States, where he had completed his own schooling and then worked for some large cattle concerns, and he had a great love for Mexico and a sadness, too, as he watched it being torn apart by economic and political problems.

By car, the trip to the ranch took hours, because there was no direct road, but it was a short hop by plane. Alberto pointed out landmarks—industry near Piedras Negras, a major power plant a few miles out of town, nut farms. He flew the outline of his ranch, stretching from the Boquillas del Carmen Highway up into the mountains. He was proud of the

Muzquiz ranch

Coahuila

improvements he'd made on the place, the tight fences, the miles and miles of white PVC pipe that made it easy to keep his cattle in water and allowed him to use pastures that might otherwise have been wasted. That pipeline saved money, too; he could show me that on the calculator, proving the amount of diesel fuel he had saved by eliminating the extra pumps and man-hours necessary to tend them.

We landed and taxied under the shelter. Lucio, the foreman, was already there with a truck. The first topic, as always with ranchers, was rain. Except for the high country, the storms that week seemed to have circled the ranch, leaving measurable amounts higher in the mountains and lower on the flat land that stretched back toward Piedras Negras.

From the air, we had seen that the cattle Alberto had come to check for shipping were penned and waiting. So we unloaded the plane and drove to the pens. They were full of big Beefmaster steers. We walked slowly into the herd, and Alberto pointed out how fat they were for having come through a dry summer. The breed was perfect for his country; when times got tough they didn't mind foraging for shrubs and even prickly pear cactus.

The air smelled of creosote and chemicals. The cowboys had opened up the dip tanks and were ready to run the steers through; it would be the final tick-dipping before they were trucked to the inspection station in Piedras Negras. Alberto climbed atop the chute he had designed and built of welded steel pipe—a system as efficient as his network of water lines. From above he could regulate the speed of the cattle as they plunged into the vat and watch to make sure that the dipping was complete. Finally, after the last steer had gone through and they stood in the drying pen, dripping the whitish liquid and looking smaller with their hair plastered down, Alberto was confident he would have no problems taking them across the border.

Later, sitting with me on the cool veranda of the old ranch house, Cornelia Muzquiz talked about growing up in Mexico. She was fine-boned and pretty in a delicate way, and drawing the chairs up to a small table, she moved with an easy, natural grace. Her early years, which had come at the end of an era in Mexico, might have been from a storybook tale. "I was born in Mexico and grew up in an old hacienda that belonged to my grandfather," she said. "It was a beautiful old place in the country with lots of servants. There were huge gardens. We had a golf course, a swimming pool, everything you could imagine."

The hacienda stood near the town of Nueva Rosita, fifty or sixty miles southeast of the ranch, where the American Smelting and Refining Company had an operation. She had been allowed to attend the company school, which was conducted in English, with the children of the Anglo employees. She studied there until the seventh grade. Then she went away to boarding school, finishing her education in Virginia and Texas. "I was raised in an American-type home and spent time with a group of Americans connected with the mines. They did ordinary American things. They

Cornelia Muzquiz

had Saturday night suppers and movies and clubs. I went to the Brownies just like any normal American girl would."

She confessed that she enjoyed having access to both lives. "I like living in Eagle Pass and still being so close to this culture as well. We have Mexico at our doorstep, but we also have the United States and all its convenience—its McDonalds, its supermarkets, air-conditioning, TV, and phone service. I am able to own land, pay taxes, and vote. I like that."

A rifle shot came echoing down out of the hills. Alberto had taken Alberto Junior up there to do some shooting. Cornelia paused until the sound died out. It reminded her how much their three children were products of the border, of the two cultures. "Our kids have two lives, two worlds to live in—the ranch and the city. They are completely bilingual. I speak English to them, which is natural for me, and their father speaks Spanish to them, which is natural to him. It's something they can't really get in school."

As if to confirm this, we listened while Sara, their youngest child, scolded her miniature dachshund in English to keep him from going into the kitchen, and then called to the cook in Spanish to ask for a glass of water. She slipped from language to language with perfect ease.

Charlie and Chavela Sellers, two Anglos who owned a neighboring ranch to the north, had heard the Muzquiz's plane circling to land and decided to drive down for a visit. There was some routine ranch business to discuss, after which a swimming party was organized for the following afternoon. Cornelia talked them into staying for supper.

Jaime, the cook, built a hot mesquite fire in the backyard. When it had burned down to a bed of hot coals, he threw a grate over them and brought out a plateful of thick Kansas City steaks.

Over dinner, I asked Chavela how she had come to live in Mexico.

"I'm a Mexican," she replied.

In fact, she was second-generation Mexican. Her father had been born in Mexico; her grandfather, an Englishman, had arrived in the area via Argentina, Australia, and New Zealand. Her mother had been born in Marfa, Texas, and had moved into Coahuila to teach in the same American school Cornelia had attended.

Charlie Sellers had come over from Texas to manage a vast ranch near Chavela's father's place. "I've lived here so long I feel more Mexican than anything else," he said.

But he and Chavela didn't meet in this part of the country. "It was a funny thing," she laughed. "Even though Charlie was running a ranch right across the mountain from ours, I had to go to Mexico City so he would pay attention to me."

"Pretty expensive romance," Charlie grinned. He had a thin wind-honed face with a line across his forehead where his hat fit.

Border life was a topic that interested Chavela. She admitted that because of their situation she had thought a lot about it. "I really feel that it's a world in itself. I don't think people who live outside of it, on either side of the river, quite realize how different and interrelated life here is. The people go back and forth the way they would with any city divided by a river. We've always lived this way, in two countries that are really one country. And we do love going to the other side, just like any other of these Mexicans, but I don't know if we could ever adjust to living there. At least I don't know if I could." And Charlie was shaking his head.

I mentioned that, as unlikely as it sounded, there had been some talk of shutting down the border.

Alberto spoke up, his humor evident: "It would help a lot of us in the selfish sense that we could get some good help back. Most of the good ranch cowboys go to the other side."

"Yes," Chavela said, "but it would hurt the lower classes, the population in general."

"That's true," agreed Alberto, serious now. "The border acts like an escape valve, letting the people go over and work, reducing the pressure. Especially now with the peso so low, they can earn much more over there. According to the figures, if a man was only making ten dollars a day in the

States, he would be making at least four times what he could make here. I had a cowboy leave here and go to work at the polo grounds in San Antonio. I heard he's getting something like twelve dollars an hour. That would almost make him a millionaire here."

"You can't blame them for going," said Chavela. "They never have a feeling of getting anywhere in Mexico. They work to eat. Anybody gets sick and tired of that kind of situation."

Charlie cleared his throat to speak. Up to that time he had merely sipped his ice tea and listened. "Well, I hope they never stop them all from going into the States. It would really hurt Mexico, especially right now. It would be disastrous and leave Mexico with this tremendous burden. Besides, I don't think it's really hurting the United States. There is so much of this labor that goes into the United States to do work that Americans really don't want to do. I don't think they're taking that many jobs away from the Americans."

Most of the arguments I had heard on that subject were from politicians with an ax to grind for this or that special interest group. However, one morning in San Diego as I was leaving the motel where I'd spent the night, I noticed two men near my car pawing through a dumpster for aluminum cans. Scruffy, in their thirties, they had the bleached out look of California drifters. They saw me and asked for spare change. One of them, whose name was Dave, said, "Believe me, man, I really hate panhandling like this. But I can't get a job."

I asked what kind of work he did.

"I usually work as a dishwasher," he said, "but that bunch of fucking Mexicans coming across are taking all the jobs. They'll work cheaper than us. And they never heard of a forty-hour week."

Early the following morning, Alberto and I drove out to see some young horses he was keeping on a remote part of the ranch. Once we had passed the hangar with the airplane and gone through the gate, there was no evidence of the supercivilization that governed this ranch. As was to happen for the rest of that day, we gradually slipped back in time to a point at which the modern world would appear only in brief flashes before it was swallowed up in a kind of timelessness. Alberto, too, was a different person from the man with the airplane or the man with the calculator; that morning, he even wore a different hat, this one of felt and creased in a style that went back years.

He began pointing out various brush and plants in the pastures: huisache, black brush, white brush, chapote, chiles petin, creosote brush, lechuguilla, candelia, and purple sage. He stopped the pickup to show me a nopal with bites taken out of it; sometimes a cow had been forced to eat it. Farther on, we looked at the sotol, their tall flaglike stalks knocked down and chewed for food.

We found a goatherd on a hillside. He raised the staff he had cut and trimmed from a young mesquite and then came twisting down through the brush to the truck. Only to say *"Buenos dias,"* softly, shyly, and then stand

quietly staring at us. He turned his huarache uncomfortably in the dirt while Alberto asked questions about the feed and the goats. A couple of miles farther we stopped at the hut where the goatherd's family lived—the wife who had just washed her hair and was letting it dry in the sun, the boy and girl who may only have been to town once in their lives.

The next time we stopped, Alberto showed me on the map where we were. He pointed out the road to Boquillas del Carmen, a solid line giving way to a faint broken one, indicating that it was unimproved. He confessed that as long as he'd lived in this country he had never followed it all the way to Rio Bravo del Norte, the Rio Grande. And he decided then, on the spur of the moment, that we would do it.

From Alberto's Rancho La Rosita, the highway took us past Los Pintos, San Jeronimo, El Infante, La Babia, and La Questa, ranches or miniscule settlements hidden in the hills, to where the pavement ended. The road that swung north to Boquillas del Carmen turned abruptly to gravel. Within a few kilometers, that gave way to a very coarse gravel, and a few kilometers farther it degenerated to rocks the size of grapefruits and small melons. There were places where the main-traveled track veered off the roadbed to avoid washed-out spots, dodged through the mesquite for a short distance, then swerved sharply back up to the stones. No matter how rough and forbidding the road was, it cut a beautiful straight line into the smokey distance where the mountains of the Big Bend shimmered blue and gray.

Miles from Boquillas, the left front tire started going flat. The truck was propane-powered, and Alberto used a hose from the propane tank to keep the tire inflated. We came to a roadside stop and considered pulling in and changing the tire, but there was something ominous about the place. Three well-kept four-wheel-drive vehicles sat in front, and a couple of men lurked in the doorways, dark hats shadowing their faces. They might have been smugglers, fugitives, desperados who worked this area of the border where bootleggers used to keep their stills and float booze across the river in animal skins into the United States.

Once, we pulled over to allow a pickup approaching us on the narrow road to pass. As is customary in places where only a few vehicles are met, the driver stopped to pass the time of day. Partly it was curiosity, partly the desire to talk. The farmer, his wife, four children, and a baby goat were on their way to Muzquiz. They were dressed in their best clothes, probably planning to see a movie once they had disposed of the goat.

Closer to the border, *ejidos* had grown up close to the hillsides, taking their livelihood—God knows how—from the parched dry stretches of rocks and brush. The heat had increased. Houses stood silent, lengths of fabric to discourage flies blowing slightly in their open doorways. Animals huddled in the narrow midday shade. No people were visible until we came around a bend in the road and saw a string of thin, scruffy burros bringing tourists up from the river to spend an hour in the little town.

Boquillas del Carmen was a small, forlorn-looking town that seemed

Goatherd,
Coahuila

to have been carved out of the same stone that lined the walls of the gorge through which the Rio Grande ran. We had lunch on the shaded patio of a tiny cafe and then set out to explore the town. The man who might have repaired the slow leak in our tire had gone across the river for the day. But we had plenty of propane to keep pumping it up. In a tiny store, shuttered and dark because of the heat, half a dozen men sat around drinking tequila. One young man was waiting for dark to swim the river and go back to the oil field job he had in Odessa, Texas. He had been in Muzquiz on vacation with his family, and his father had ridden the bus down with him. Now he would have to wait two days until the bus

Boquillas del
Carmen,
Coahuila

returned to take him back to Muzquiz. Alberto offered to drive him as far as the ranch and let him hitch from there.

The truck had a crew cab with a second seat, and the old man, already drunk, climbed in the back. He had brought a paper cup full of tequila, which he kept sipping. He also had a pint bottle under his jacket and each time the cup was empty, he would go through the tedious operation of refilling it. While the truck banged and rattled along the road, the old man held the cup between his knees, just tight enough but not so tight he would crush it, uncapped the tequila, poured the cup full, capped the tequila, and hid it under his coat again. He had begun a kind of talking

Boquillas del Carmen, Coahuila

Boquillas del Carmen, Coahuila

song to himself and sometimes broke out with a half bar or so that we could hear. "I just hope he doesn't start throwing up—" Alberto said.

After a few miles we encountered a cattle truck going just fast enough to send a cloud of boiling white dust back at us. Alberto honked and honked, trying to get the driver to pull over and let us pass. We could see him in his side mirrors and knew that he had heard us, but he wasn't moving one way or the other. Alberto began swearing, in Spanish. He tried to slip around one side and force the truck over, but it was too big. The driver just pulled in front of us. Alberto continued to swear and the old man in the back joined him. Finally Alberto saw a clear track off to the right of the roadbed and below us about ten feet. He downshifted and sent the pickup over the side. The old man's tequila splashed out of the paper cup all over his pants. For a moment the old man's eyes were as big as baseballs and then he closed them, crossed himself and began to pray. We bounced and skidded down the embankment, remaining miraculously upright, and found the lower track. Alberto floorboarded the accelerator. The cattle truck downshifted, trying to outrun us. Alberto began to smile. We were outdistancing the truck, but there seemed no way back up the embankment to the roadbed. The pickup shuddered across the banks of a dry creek. The old man's prayers grew louder. Suddenly, up ahead there was a spot where we could get back on top. The trouble was, the cattle truck had begun to gain now. It was a grim macho contest, the Mexican male game. We crashed over the top of some small mesquite and caught the rocky track. Alberto powershifted into a lower gear, the sudden torque shooting a spray of rocks up into the wheelwells with a sound like machine-gun fire. It seemed we sailed to the top, barely ahead of the cattle truck.

Alberto did not mention the episode, nor did the old man in the back. But he had crushed his cup and was now forced to forego such finesse and drink directly from the bottle. After a few drinks to fortify himself, he remembered someone he wanted to see in a settlement along the way and asked to be let off there. Alberto watched him a moment in the mirror, then said, *"Si, señor—"*

We drove in silence until we went up a rise and through a cut in a hill. The country opened up before us and Alberto said: "This is the real Mexico."

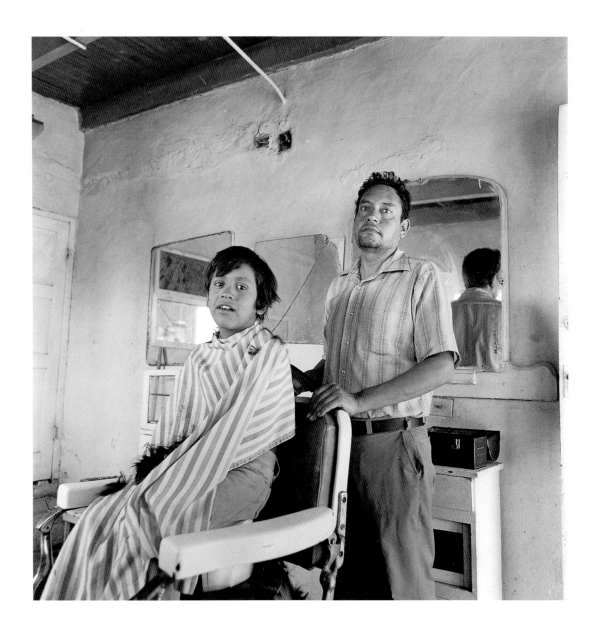

Jesus Flores Hernandez, coffin maker, Juárez

Funeral parlor, Juárez

Francisco Villa
Do, cemetery
caretaker,
Juárez

Eduardo Islas
Perea, piñata
maker, Tijuana

*Car club
member, San
Diego,
California*

Raul Trejo de Lopez, Roberto Lopez Trejo, and Yoluvina Trejo, east of Juárez, Highway 2

SMUGGLERS

A Mexican kid on a beat-up red Honda motorcycle cruised the hard wet sand at the edge of the surf near Boca Chica, the point where the Rio Grande finally ends its long swing down out of Colorado—after cutting the state of New Mexico in two and tracing the entire length of Texas—and empties wearily into the sea. It was a three-day holiday weekend, and the beach was packed with people who couldn't afford chic places like South Padre Island, people who had swarmed down from Brownsville and San Antonio with tents and sleeping bags to try and beat the heavy South Texas heat and humidity. At each group of teenagers, the kid stopped his bike. Sometimes he would ride on; sometimes he waited while one from the group trotted to a car for a billfold and there would be a transaction. He was peddling little stuff, joints and tiny bags of blow.

On another afternoon, five girls in a white Mustang crossed the bridge out of Via Acuna back into Del Rio. After watching them score on a street corner in Mexico, I tailed them, curious to see if they would be busted at the border. The agent waved them through. They drove to the parking lot in front of an H.E.B. store, where they pulled into an open area and set about trying to get high.

Over a two-night period while I was in McAllen, Texas, the local police busted a total of eighty-nine people, most of them students at two area high schools, for delivering grass or coke or both to undercover agents. The reaction was pretty low key, except for a vigorous outcry of entrapment from enraged parents.

These were all nickel-and-dimers, small-time smugglers and their accomplices, a crowd common almost everywhere along the border. And as the peso dropped and the stuff seemed easier and easier to come by— in whatever quantities—I saw more and more of them. But I was interested in contacting someone bigger, someone making more than the rent, more than gas and pocket money.

A coyote in Mexico

**Boca Chica,
Texas**

One night in San Antonio when I mentioned that I wanted to interview a smuggler with a sizeable operation, the person I was having dinner with said, "Just look for a Rolex—"

He meant, of course, the same heavy gold watch you see worn by politicians in power and high-ranking members of the Mexican police, an "Oyster" with gold links the size of a small bulldozer's tracks and almost none of the features of the digital throwaway watches from Japan. That this big, cumbersome timepiece, gaudy and ostentatious as it is, was actually worn by almost all the smugglers I finally did meet is probably more than a coincidence. In Mexico, politicians, important police, and smugglers are the people likely to have the kind of money it takes to own one and to dare wear it.

Most smugglers seem to have their finger on one pulse—their own. It quickens for two reasons: if there is money to be made, and if there is trouble.

Trouble comes mainly from two sources—the police and the competition. Because of the *mordida*, the little "bite" or bribe that makes all things possible in Mexico, the police are by far the easier to deal with; a small but regular amount of money will turn those heads away at precisely the right moment. The competition is another matter. It seems there are no lengths to which these people will not go to stop their own kind.

A story circulating in the state of Coahuila last fall told of a group of smugglers from Sinaloa, a state farther south, who had moved to the area, hoping to muscle in on some of the action. To a trained observer, which my informant certainly was, the whole thing was all too obvious. Suddenly, a Mexican with a small rancho on the banks of the Rio Grande had sold out for at least triple the going price such property would bring. The new owners trucked in a string of expensive race horses, brood mares from good bloodlines, a couple of stud horses, and set up a breeding farm. The trouble was, they were spending money faster and far more recklessly than almost anyone in the horse business could afford to do. The evidence made it clear, at least to other smugglers, that this was an obvious cover for a new drug pipeline out of Sinaloa.

People in the same business in Coahuila, who had paid to get control of the major smuggling avenue and were therefore worthy of a certain amount of respect and fear, had neither been consulted or, so it seemed, even considered. It was a brazen affront and had already created plenty of friction. Still, the consensus was that there would be no violence. The established smugglers, whether they were the Mob or not, had paid their *mordida* and would only have to alert the police—*their* police (it was hinted that this also included DEA agents on the Texas side)—that a big shipment was about to arrive for crossing. No one knew when that would be; but they could wait.

**Nogales,
Sonora**

Everyone believes the Mob is in Mexico, especially in the north, and that they control drugs and prostitution. I heard about it constantly in statements that often conflicted with and contradicted one another except

Tijuana

*Highway 2,
Mexico*

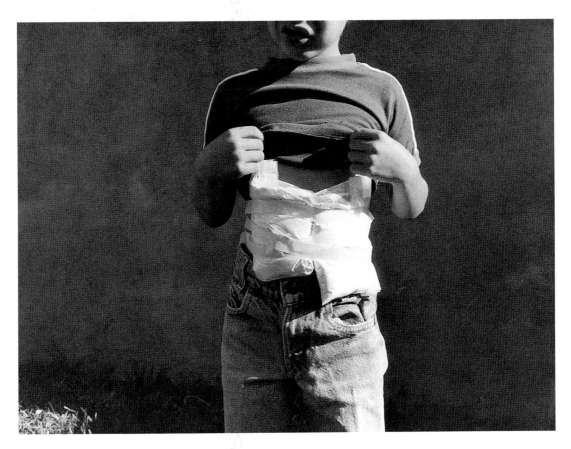

Mule, near
Tecate, Baja
California

in one respect: that the *Mafiosos* were in control. Still, these massive organized crime cartels don't always have the same effect on the immediate border as the little smuggling operations consisting of one man and two or three helpers. This area, where the volume is smaller, seems to belong mostly to the little guys.

My introduction to one of the small-time smugglers came out of Texas, but the man it concerned was a Mexican. A businessman I'd met had a friend who knew this Mexican smuggler named Jesus Lopez. A couple of calls were made, and I was given an address on a napkin from the restaurant in Del Rio where we had talked about it.

I met Jesus Lopez at night. It came after a crazy cab ride into one of the dense barrios of a border town just across the Rio Grande. In Texas, I had been told that Jesus would smuggle anything out of the United States into Mexico. I had been told, too, that he refused to go the other direction—not one joint, one ounce of coke, one *serape* would he take out of Mexico. But if someone had an order and the thing they wanted could be moved, Jesus would get it into Mexico for them. This included sheep, tractors, pipe, motors, parts, drilling rigs, anything that was portable.

The cab driver had puzzled over the address for the long time, conferred with a second driver, who raised both hands in the air and walked away, and then set out from the plaza. The cab, a Chevy with a 3-D picture of Christ in a crown of thorns pasted to the dash and two plastic saints standing just above the radio, as though they were about to dance, shuddered through potholes and zigzagged farther into the barrio. We came to a dead-end street. The exasperated driver backed out to the first cross street, careening from side to side, and tried again. Finally, he stopped the cab and disappeared into a *carniceria*. He returned muttering to himself, and we turned back in the direction from which we had come. Eventually he found the street and the house.

It was a small place—as most barrio houses are; and it was cozy—as most of them are not. You could tell the pieces of furniture that had been pirated into the country from the U.S., the ugly green recliner, the TV, the stereo; I would have seen even more in the kitchen, all the superior American appliances most Mexicans covet. Naturally, none of this showed on the outside of the house. Jesus had stayed in business precisely because he was not ostentatious. There were other reasons, of course, and those he would explain.

Jesus had one of those classic round Mexican faces, smooth and dark, with too much jowl. He greased his black hair and wet-combed it close to his scalp. And although you wouldn't exactly call him fat, he had a potbelly that kept his shirt front stretched tight enough to put a serious strain on the buttons.

Jesus was uneasy about hanging around his house with me. He didn't come out and say that, but I could feel it and see from the hard time he was having to stay seated in the recliner. He lived in a world where being careful in some areas made it possible to take chances in others. It was his respect for this rule that had made him a survivor. He rubbed his hands together and said he was hungry. He knew a place he thought I might appreciate.

His car was a late-model Ford, and he had a curious way of driving it. With the seat pushed back and his body turned against the doorpost, he steered with one hand, and continued to talk. Now that we were away from his house he was much more relaxed. He laughed and said: "This is some shithole of a town, eh?" He cruised effortlessly out of the half-paved streets that had given the cabbie so much grief. "But I like it. Why?" he asked himself and then shrugged at his own question. "I wouldn't know how to live anyplace else."

"What about the States?"

"I couldn't live over there—" he said. "I'm a Mexican."

He let that statement hang in the air briefly before he went on. "It's not easy for us in Mexico right now. The peso is shit. The government's worse. But I'm a patriot." He touched his hand to his heart and was silent for a moment. Then he showed a wide smile. "Besides, I have connections. I make a living."

He drove to a low, sprawling building a mile or so from the edge of town. If there was a sign, it was not lighted. There were a couple of Texas cars nosed up close to the entrance and a few Mexican vehicles with Frontera plates, pickups, cars, and a cattle truck. A cantina song with a blaring backup of cracked trumpets reached into the dark parking lot.

Jesus introduced me to the owner, a jovial man with a waxed gray mustache, and we were taken to a choice table.

"The food is good here," Jesus said, when we were alone. "The girls—" he turned his palm up, a gesture that told me I'd have to judge them for myself.

There were four to consider. Two were at a corner table with two Texans. A third sat at the bar with a ranchero. She was a pretty girl in brand-new ice-blue spike heels, which I took to be her most cherished possession, and a simple sheath of white satin with sequins shining on the narrow straps over nice brown shoulders. She was probably the prize. Or maybe it was the fat one who kept trying to pull her miniskirt down over knees the size of watermelons. At least it was to her that Jesus's eyes kept straying. *De gustibus*, I thought. After all, he had *bought* the green La-Z-Boy recliner.

At my first question about what he liked to call his "import" business, Jesus leaned closer and took a firm grip on the damp Corona bottle from which he'd been drinking. "The bottom line, as you like to say over there, is simple. If you want to stay in business, you take care of everyone." Each time he made a point he drew a wet line on the waxed surface of the table with the bottom of his bottle. "You pay, man. You pay the police, you pay the customs officials. You pay every last little fucker of a public official who might ever get in your way. And sometimes you still have trouble. But with everyone else on your side, a little more money will take care of that, too."

Was it so easy? This Mexican *savoir faire* had always baffled me. The ones who had it seemed to live from the very top of the world. Their last white shirt would be starched and pressed, and they would toss their last peso to the shoeshine kid.

"It is never easy, señor. But in Mexico, the *mordida* is the way of life. I pay off everyone. I keep them on a retainer. It's not big, but in a poor country it's enough."

"How do you find your customers?"

"They find me. I check them out and choose the ones I am certain I can satisfy."

Why, I wanted to know, was there so much trafficking in ordinary goods.

Jesus took a long drink of beer, a string of bubbles dancing up the neck of the bottle. "Mexico has some unfortunate import laws. They were made to protect us as a country, to help us overcome our poverty. But very often what is produced here is inferior, or there is not enough of it, or it has to be trucked all the way up here from Mexico City."

When a new song started, the ranchero guided the girl in white to the dance floor. His style was intense. He let his hand slip down to her ass and pressed his body against hers. She stared over his shoulder, responding enough to keep him interested but mostly just staying out of his way, trying to protect her precious shoes.

Generous plates of *carne asada*, tender filets of beef prepared the Mexican way, and *refritos* arrived with a wrapped stack of tortillas. Jesus fell to eating, using his fork and a rolled corn tortilla.

I was curious about his nickname, the Midnight Bandit. The question brought a smile to his face. "Only the gringos call me that," he laughed, still chewing. "How did I get it? I don't know. Maybe because I cross everything at night. I bring it over between midnight and four in the morning. I could do it in the daylight, you know. But I feel more comfortable under the cover of darkness. I think it's because I understand the night. It is a home to different people. We understand each other."

In Mexican towns all along the border I had heard rumors of revolutionary activities. I mentioned to Jesus that in Brownsville I had heard of guns being brought into Mexico; there was speculation that these were going to forces that were beginning to build in the north.

Jesus seemed unfazed by this information. He chewed a moment. "Yes, guns do come across. Some of them go on to Central America."

"But some stay?"

He dabbed at a pool of meat juice with his tortilla. "I have heard of an operation back in the hills. Young men are coming to these guerrilla camps on the weekend and being paid American dollars to train with weapons developed by the American military. But I don't think they are brought in by the CIA. America is not smart enough to recognize how much it needs Mexico. It would sooner fight phantom wars with phantom troops farther south."

"How long will it be?"

"You mean if it comes?" he smiled.

"Yes," I conceded. "Three years, five?"

"Yes—or overnight. After all, how long did it take Villa to mass his army in 1913—five or six months? So who can say?"

Arturo Galván was also a Mexican. He showed up at the corrugated steel hangar at exactly the time we had set for our meeting. Leaning against the front of the building, he watched a couple of small airplanes taxi into line

Smuggler checking airplane before takeoff

for takeoff. He was a slender man in tan saddle pants and a pair of powder-blue ostrich cowboy boots. He smelled of the kind of designer cologne sold in duty-free tourist shops, and when he spoke his smile was edged with dental gold. His crisp white shirt had been starched and carefully ironed, but the initials monogrammed onto the pocket—EJB—did not in any way add up to Arturo Galván, the name I had been given.

Ironically, we were standing less than fifty yards from the U.S. Customs office at the airport. "Do you want to go someplace else to talk?" I asked.

"No—this will be all right. Now, just tell me what you want to know."

I could see that he was not bothered. He folded his arms and spoke

*Hangars,
Texas*

*Landing
strip
in Texas*

with a cool detachment—in English that was almost perfect, except for syntax and a slight accent that wasn't right for that part of the country.

"I never do anything on the ground," he said, stating the one and *only* rule that apparently governed his business. "I always use airplanes."

"What plane do you like best," I asked. "I mean, what's the best one for the cargo and the country?"

"The airplane I like is a DC-4," he stroked his chin as he talked. "It is big, and it can take off and land in a very short space. And it is dependable."

No, he did not always own the plane or the merchandise. Sometimes, if he felt he could trust the person who wanted to hire him, he hired out as a pilot. Then, as often as not, he did not know what he was smuggling, and he didn't care. Either way he did it, for himself or someone else, the pay was good. As a pilot, he could earn twelve to fifteen hundred dollars a trip—sometimes more—depending on the deal. He could usually make two trips a night, if they got moving early enough and there were no problems.

"Where do you usually fly from?"

"Texas," he replied, keeping it loose and general.

"What's your method of operation?"

"What do you mean *method?*"

"How do you get the stuff, whatever it is, and how do you get it across?"

"It is always different."

"Can you describe the last trip you made?" I asked, trying to push him into something concrete.

He stopped watching the taxi strip. His eyes were fixed on me. "We loaded the plane in Texas."

"At an airport?"

"Yes. We kept the plane inside the hangar until the final cargo was in. We took off at about eight-thirty in the night and crossed over into Mexico."

"Did you file a flight plan?"

"Not personally."

"But one was filed—by someone?"

"Yes. By someone."

"Did it include Mexico?"

"I don't know that," he said. "I was instructed to fly to San Luis Potosí. It was not an operation I had anything to do with—except as a pilot. But it was well thought out. It had to be, the plane was full. If something went wrong these people would lose a lot. I had worked for them before, so I knew I would get paid. Those are the kind of jobs I don't mind taking. The risk isn't much."

A Piper Pacer with a Mexican identification number taxied up to the marked pad in front of the small customs building. An agent carrying a clipboard approached the plane. Arturo was aware of the agent, but he never really looked at him.

"Did you know what you were carrying?"

"No, not that time."

"It could have been guns, right?"

"It could have been," he agreed. "But guns would have been heavier. I'd have felt it from the cockpit."

"Did you fly to an airport?"

"No. You almost never do that—not in Mexico."

"Where did you fly to, then?"

As if pondering how much he should tell me, Arturo paused and watched a silver Beechcraft idle onto the runway. Lurching against the brake, it revved its engine for a long time, the sound changing when the prop was feathered. A cloud of dust blew back into the grass and weeds.

"We landed in the desert country this side of Ciudad San Luis Potosí. They had the strip marked with *bombas*, those round kerosene lamps they use on construction sites. I set the plane down without circling. A crew of men was waiting to unload the plane. I kept the right engine running and stayed in the cockpit with the copilot. In less than an hour, we were back in the air."

"And that's all there was to it?" I asked.

"Not exactly. We made a second trip that same night. I was paid almost three thousand dollars."

He smiled then, for the first time. "A man can live well in Mexico on those kind of wages—especially with the devaluation."

Months later, from the point of view of a decrepit small-town taxi strip at twilight, I would look back on my meetings with both Jesus Lopez and Arturo Galván as simple, sane, and ridiculously safe.

I'd heard plenty of stories about fancy tricked-out airplanes flown by the major smugglers with ties to the Mob or the Mexican government. The plane I was in was hardly one of those; it wasn't even in the class of the huge DC-4 tail-dragger described by Arturo. It was a single-engine fleet craft, gutted down to the bulkheads, except for the front seats, and stripped of anything not absolutely essential to flight. This left a large cavity that could be filled almost back to the tail. The throaty sound of the engine betrayed the fact that either it had been tampered with enough to increase the horsepower significantly or the original engine had been ripped out and replaced with an oversize model.

Jimmy Williams kept the plane cranked and vibrating fitfully for what seemed a very long time. He watched the gauges and checked every detail. Finally satisfied, he cut the throttle and settled into his seat. "I don't ever intend to be left over in that godforsaken country of theirs just because my goddamn airplane quit on me," he chuckled and released the brake.

Jimmy was not what I had expected. He lacked the dash of an Indiana Jones or the cool savvy of any of the hotshot smugglers regularly shown on "Miami Vice." He didn't even have the flare of the two Mexicans I had interviewed. With his saddle-blanket sports jacket and balding head, he had the look of a man who would sell you a pre-owned car (which would be the word he'd use) or a discount TV—and the latter was part of what he actually did move on these night trips into Mexico.

As soon as we were airborne we swung to the west, where the last of the sunlight was like a long brush stroke of red paint on the horizon, with the Rio Grande another brush stroke of silver stretching out until it disappeared into the dusk. We were up barely ten minutes when Jimmy cut the power, banked sharply to the right, and began a fast sliding descent into the darkness. Just then a ragged line of lights flashed on, marking a ranch landing strip in the middle of nowhere.

"Just sit where you are," Jimmy said, after we'd rolled to a stop. His easy facade had fallen away; he was strictly business now. He pushed open the door and waited for the prop to crank down. "No need makin' these boys here any more nervous than they already are."

A rented truck pulled alongside the plane. Jimmy and two other men loaded boxes through the cargo doors, filling the space behind the seats to the ceiling. A second truck had aimed its headlights at the plane. I could make out the gray composition-plastic handle of a serious military weapon sticking out from under the front of Jimmy's seat. It gave me the first of a number of unsettling moments I would have on this trip.

Nogales,
Sonora

Tijuana

With its load, the plane moved a lot slower. The runway lights had been snuffed out as soon as we were down; now we took off with only the landing lights of the plane raking out through the stiff short grass. We headed west again, into a slate-colored sky, never gaining very much altitude, slipped across the dull ribbon of the river into Mexico, and then started to climb. At nine thousand feet, he cut back the throttle and switched off the strobe markers.

It was up here that Jimmy had chosen to be interviewed, as if it might somehow insure his anonymity. He talked freely, assuring me that before the devaluation of the peso, he had smuggled absolutely nothing. The thought had never even occurred to him.

But that single event in Mexican economics, with its direct, devastating impact on the border, had resulted in his losing his business, which—although it had been on the American side—relied heavily on Mexican trade. People could no longer afford to come across the bridge and buy in Texas, at least not the kind of merchandise he had been selling. He had actually made his first flight across with the goods he was trying to liquidate in order to meet his notes at the bank.

"It wasn't even my idea," he said. "This guy out of Mexico City showed up one day and made me an offer I couldn't refuse. He said something about this dude who could probably get the stuff across. Fuck that noise, I told him. I can fly the shit in if you can receive it."

He had meant to stop right there, with that first load. Except the money was good—in fact, it was about the only money available along the border at that time. He could still get the stuff wholesale and the flying was nothing. "I flew some missions in Vietnam that make these goddamn little pissant trips into Mexico seem like a cakewalk."

I asked if he ever flew anything *out* of Mexico.

His comeback was quick, as if he'd expected the question: "You mean drugs, right?"

"Yes—"

"I tell you what, Jack, I wouldn't touch that shit. The business is too damn dirty. Drugs is never just a deal between me and you. It's always something bigger. Like syndicates. And governments. Now, bodies—yes. That's a whole 'nuther story. I've brought in a few loads of Central Americans and what have you. It's never just your regular wetbacks looking for a job tending lawn or something. These are family deals. They've got people waiting for them in the States, and they've got the dough to pay for the trip."

Jimmy sat up suddenly, scooting his seat ahead a notch to be closer to the controls. Once again we began dipping into the darkness. In the distance, a set of headlights came on, then a second set. They marked opposite ends of a road where we were meant to land.

"So what keeps you in it," I wanted to know, "the money?"

"When I first started, it was the money," he said. "I don't mind telling you there's lots of bucks in this business. But there's something else about it that gets to you. Most people don't like to admit it, but parts of that war over there were fun. I don't mean the killing. There were just times when you'd fly into something so damn hairy that it'd make your asshole pucker up like a fuckin' prune or something."

He laughed. In the greenish lights from the instrument panel, his face had become an eerie mask.

"It's the danger, then—" I suggested.

"Yeah. There's really not that much danger up here." He patted the steering wheel. "The Mexicans don't have any kind of air force to speak of. Hell, they probably can't even fly half the stuff we've given them. But I'll tell you what," he said, jerking his head toward the lighted road, which was now to our right, "you sure as hell never know what the show's going to be down there. Somebody might've fucked up."

And as we were gliding toward the first set of headlights, passing low over the cab of the pickup and getting ready to set down, I realized that he was right. Until then I had never considered what might be waiting for us.

I knew two things for certain: I was in a plane full of contraband; and I was flying with a professional smuggler. I could just see myself trying to tell the Federal Judicial Police of Mexico, who had a reputation for being about half as nice as a squad of Nazi storm troopers, that I was innocent, that I was just a photographer, a guy writing a book.

And at that moment, with the plane dropping toward the road and the wings dancing uneasily in the air currents, I did know what Jimmy had meant about that puckering feeling.

REFUGEES

No questions asked," they said, in effect. It was the "unofficial" position of the people of God. If someone down and out needed help, they offered all they could. That meant beds, clothing, food. When it went beyond that there was no one who wanted to say how far.

This particular place in El Paso was called Annunciation House. It had gained a reputation across the border in Mexico and, farther south, into Central America. People passed through; they left their stories; they carried the name. It was a warm, safe place for people who had known cold, hunger, fear, and pain.

The building itself had had a string of lives as disparate as those of its guests. It had served as warehouse, office building, plumbing supply, and half a dozen other things before it became a shelter, a stopping place, a starting point, a springboard to a new life. Those were the good stories; sometimes the house served only as a brief haven before apprehension and deportation.

Everywhere you looked there was evidence of its strange past. Doors led to nowhere, the patches of paint revealed its configuration in another time, add-on plumbing ran along the ceiling and down the walls. The furniture, like the clothing and food, was mostly handout stuff—cots and bunk beds and double beds and those foldout couches that double as beds; tables, desks, and unmatched chairs stood about in no certain arrangement.

Still, no one seemed uncomfortable. It was warm and dry. There was a spirit in the house that held it all together. And there was hope.

They knew, of course, that the Migra knew they were there. The green-and-white vans cruised these streets day and night. Normally the agents did nothing about it. Today there had been a bust outside the front door and another at the airport, as if the crackdown had been specifically targeted, and that had slashed the population in half.

Luis Perez
Rincon, refugee
in Texas

It had come as a shock. But both that and the fear had worn off soon enough; these were people who had known worse. And by evening the young kids, Salvadorans, Guatamalans, Nicaraguans, Mexicans, were out on the tarmac playing a fast game of basketball.

The workers were all volunteers. The majority were college kids from New York, Chicago, Kansas City, who had felt a vocation that wasn't strong enough for priesthood but who nonetheless wanted to do *something*, to fill some empty spaces left by a couple of decades of upper-middle-class living.

"School just didn't seem that concrete anymore," said one young man, warming his fingers around a chipped coffee mug. "I wanted to do something real." And it had been real, enough so that it had increased his appetite for more. "After this I'm going to move on to Mexico or Central America, where the need is even greater...."

Some of them were doing it out of a conviction, others were there (and in the other places I visited) for the thrill. After all, this was the underground, an outpost at the edge of the law, that murky area where law and religion separate over basic issues. And these volunteers had no other revolution to go to. It was an opportunity to dress the part, to talk it, to live a certain side of it. For this they would even swab out the toilets.

Just before nine, someone knocked at the door. It was unlocked. A young Nicaraguan walked in, apprehensive but smiling. He wore a cowboy hat and carried a tightly packed bag. Protruding from the outside pocket was a stereo album. He said he needed a room for the night. "How did you hear about us?" one of the workers asked in second-year college Spanish. He had been told about the house by a Mexican who had waded the river with him a couple of hours before. Word traveled.

After dinner, the big living room filled up. People talked, read, listened to a portable radio. Under it all was something else, a kind of nervousness that no one seemed to want to let out. At one point a car door closed outside and a Venezualan in his early thirties jumped. "Ha ha, *tiene miedo—*" one of the Guatamalans accused. You're afraid, *hombre*. A pointing finger. Then everyone in the room laughed and were suddenly more relaxed, releasing the tension that had built in the hours since the bust.

I was given a place to sleep in a dorm that night. It was a room full of bunk beds and could accommodate eighteen bodies (it was interesting that both the God squad and the Border Patrol use the same terminology). There was almost none of the clutter of ordinary life. The aliens carried very little—the photograph of a girlfriend, a radio, a rosary. The heater was a gas-fired industrial suspended from the ceiling on steel straps; it came on periodically with the force of a noisy storm.

Lights-out was 10:30. There were a few jokes. The Nicaraguan who had just come in was first to sleep, his quiet snoring betraying total exhaustion. Gradually the chatter stopped. Replacing it was a noisy still-ness that grew and grew as these young minds ground through their memories and added another day to the files of their lives. It seemed to build until there was a furious roaring in the silent, solitary dark of the night.

Gradually there were more sleepers. I listened to the uneasy tossing and turning, the ancient bunks groaning under the shift of weight. And gradually I became aware of a peculiar smell, the smell of sulphur. And I realized that it was fear, the curious smell of fear that percolates to the surface of the skin.

Most genuine successes in the area of aid along the border seem to wheel around an individual. In the case of Annunciation House the individual was Ruben Garcia. Annunciation House had fulfilled a dream he'd had for years. But it had gone beyond what he had originally envisioned for the poor and homeless. It had reshaped the dream as it discovered the need it was to serve, and Ruben had allowed himself to go along more as a witness to and custodian of the idea.

The next morning, after a breakfast of chorizos and eggs and hot tortillas, I went down to Ruben's office to interview him about the house. It seemed that all the volunteers had suddenly discovered something pressing they needed to do in the office.

Ruben, tall for a Hispanic and slender in his corduroy jeans, blue shirt, and lightweight sweater, had a precise way of expressing himself. This was made more pronounced by the way the volunteers, now no longer pretending to be busy, hung on each word. They had found more here than a service job to help atone for some middle-class guilt. In Ruben they had found a guru.

RUBEN'S STORY

Annunciation House was born initially out of the desire to come down and share our lives with the poor. I was working for the youth department for the diocese of El Paso, and I talked to a number of young adults, some of whom were in college, others of whom were working, and asked them if they would like to explore the possibility of spending some time doing this work. At that point, of course, we didn't have a building; in fact, we didn't know exactly where it would actually start. I knew about the existence of this building and in the back of my mind my hope was that the building would be available. So a group of about ten or eleven young adults began to gather, and we got together on a once-a-week basis for well over a year until this building became available—anyway, the second floor of the building. So I went to talk to the bishop and the bishop said yes, you can use the building for what you want to use it for, and yes you can use it without any strings attached. I told him that I was asking him for the building but that I did not want the work to be under the diosese, that it was going to be separate, that it was something we were going to try and do on our own.

So once I had the building I came back to this group of people and said it is time to make a decision, who wants to take that step? Besides

*Central
American in
Annunciation
House*

*Central
American in
Annunciation
House*

myself there were four other young adults who came forward to help start it. On February 3, 1978, we moved into the second floor of the building. And that is how Annunciation House got started.

Throughout the entire year that we met to do the planning it never once occurred to us that we would actually take people into the building. We talked about using it as a place out of which to operate. We foresaw the possibility of having a clothing bank, having a food pantry, and having different kinds of classes, such as English classes, which would be of benefit to the people in the area.

We saw most of our work in relationship to the people here in the barrio because we are right on the fringes of El Paso's largest barrio. We saw our work just making ourselves available to people who lived here and letting them let us know how it was that we could be of service to them. We wanted an experience that would allow us to live simply, to depend on the grace of God for our existence. We didn't have any funding source, we never have had any funding source, we did not want a funding source. We wanted the freedom of not having to worry about reporting back to or satisfying someone who funds you. And at the same time we wanted to have to deal with the experience of not having a regular income and all of that.

It wasn't until we were actually here that the possibility of taking people in came about. A couple of months after we moved in there was a phone call from a lady who belonged to one of the prayer groups. She asked if we would take in a sixteen-year-old runaway who had been living in California. He had come to this area, and they had bumped into him in one of the churches. He had been hustling. So we took him in.

It was as a result of that that we said to ourselves, look there's probably other people who need a place to stay. Maybe we need to get some beds. So we began to pray for beds. Sure enough, we got a bed; and Scott had a bed.

We thought: if there is one, there's probably others and decided it would be good to have other beds. So we prayed for another bed, and another bed came, and sure there was another person—Robert—and another person. So that's how it happened.

One of our goals from the very beginning had been to try and focus in on those people who had the least resources available to them. For that reason we have always gravitated toward the undocumented here in this surrounding area. They have been the majority of our guests. We used to take in a lot more residents and citizens than we do now. We've never done any publicity for the house. We've never gone out and put signs up or said we're here or any of that kind of stuff. We've just done the work, and little by little the people have come to know about the house and to know to come here.

People entering the United States with no papers, no documentation, people who are out on the street, destitute, are the people who come to us. They are in this condition either because they never had anything—

Central American in El Paso, Texas

Guatemalan in Annunciation House

they were poor and fleeing that poverty and their hope is that they can live—or because they might have had money but they were robbed on the way. Whatever the reason, when they come here they are looking for just the absolute basic necessities to exist because it is survival time.

Within that general category of people there are some who come from politically sensitive areas—Central America and some countries in South America as well. They come, and their story is a little bit different in that they feel that they have a political need, a problem that could result in some form of persecution should they be returned. Fortunately we are able to assist them in actually filing the forms for political asylum, filling them out—and this is for both the United States and Canada. We have a network of contacts here locally, attorneys that we can go through in getting their applications filed and then assisting them to the point where they can take responsibility for their own case and build their own relationship with their attorney and continue from that point on.

This whole asylum thing is a very lengthy process. Really, what we're doing is just getting it started. The conclusion is something that is going to be way down the road—especially in the case of asylum in the United States. We see the conclusion come much faster for those that apply to Canada. In a number of cases, we've seen them get accepted into Canada, we've taken them to the airport, and in that way we have seen a physical conclusion to our part of it. For them it is just the beginning because it is the start of a new life.

What we can do all depends on the individual. If that individual seeks asylum, then he must be willing to talk and to have his story become part of the public record—and there could be danger in that. There is always a possibility that the information these people give could make its way back to their home countries and cause problems for relatives. So they need to think those decisions through carefully.

Our commitment from the beginning is to the Gospel. We're not overly concerned with upward mobility and whether or not we will be chairpersons of boards and so on. The Gospel is our guide. And I quickly have to add: we do our work very imperfectly. The minute you start speaking about the Gospel, people have all kinds of expectations about how you should live. And I would be the first to admit that we do it very imperfectly. And with many failings. But we want to share our lives, and we want to be of service to those who need us—especially the poor. So we do whatever we can.

I believe very strongly in what St. Thomas More used to say about Christians needing to use and make use of everything within the law that is available to them, to avoid, to dodge, to get time, et cetera. That they need to make use of all of that and that they need to be very bright and thoughtful in the way that they function. But the bottom line nonetheless remains that you live with the Gospel. So I guess my concern is that we not be careless or reckless in what we do, that we be humble, and that we recognize that there is much that we cannot do, that there is much that is

not within our power to change. But that we also have the courage to say yes to whatever is asked of us when it is possible. What implications there are to that only God knows. I don't know the future.

I have never been in the seminary. I am a lay person; I have been a lay person all my life. I know why I came here, why I am here. I know what it is I am trying to do, what it is that I feel I've been called to do. And to the extent that anyone is responding to that convinces me there is a certain kinship of spirits that binds us. I like the expression "God on the border" because there is a special presence here in the way God manifests himself or herself among the people and in their journeys and pilgrimages.

For example, over the years I have been guardian to ten or eleven minors; usually these young people have been teenagers who come into the U.S. from Central America. Which means that many times they have come up unaccompanied, that their family has sent them out because they feared for them. They have been detained here at the border, and the immigration judges have been willing to release them into my care.

For me to function on their behalf and for them to function has meant taking out guardianship. Then they could be put into school, and I could begin to help with their cases for political asylum. Right now it happens that I am guardian for six of them, five of whom are living with me right now, here at the house. The youngest of these is eight years old, a little boy who is here with his brothers and sisters. He is from El Salvador. His mother was assassinated; his father was—disappeared. For all intents and purposes, their parents were also orphans, and there was no extended family to which they could turn.

The other children I have been guardian to are now living in different places. One is now in Los Angeles. After almost two years we were able to trace down an uncle whose wife had a sister who married an American citizen and who, by virtue of that marriage, became a citizen and immigrated. So he went off to live with them. For another one we were able to trace down a brother; he is now living in Houston with that brother. Two of them are in Albuquerque, and both of these are going to school. I pretty well keep tabs on where they are, but as they begin to reach adult age— and you have to keep in mind that "adult" in Central Americanese is very different from "adult" in Americanese. In Central America you are an adult when you reach fifteen, sixteen. You are pretty well functioning almost 100 percent on your own behalf, and you are given that freedom within the

family. So when they have gotten a little bit older, they have charted out their own course.

I've sent them out, but I haven't had the feeling of a father watching children go away. First of all, I've never been a father, so I don't know what fathers feel when their children leave. Certainly a closeness has formed between me and each child, and that closeness has varied, depending on how long the minor has lived here with me. But they do become a part of my family in a very real sense. And when they leave there is a sense of loss, yet there is a sense of real joy because they are taking some steps forward, and a real sense of satisfaction in knowing that I think the steps that they are taking are probably a little bit more stable than if they'd never been here. They've learned what is important. They've lived in a place where they didn't have to worry about where the next meal was going to come from. They didn't have to worry about whether they were going to freeze that night. When those basic feelings are taken care of, then people have energy to ask questions about who am I. What do I want to do with my life? And do I want to work? How can I work? When people do not have those things, then they can only live one day at a time, one meal at a time; it is survival only. They cannot see beyond the next meal. And it is really gratifying to see that I have been a part of that happening in somebody else's life.

I remember putting one of the kids I had staying with me into public schools here, in high school. He was seventeen. He had never been inside of a school before in his entire life. I could not help but reflect that he is a peasant from El Salvador (I'd had a chance to visit his family, an incredibly poor family, the family that literally struggles and uses all its energy just to eat) and he suddenly had security, and he was going to go to school and get started. It was tremendously moving to see that this had come about for him.

Today, he speaks English; he's got an accent and still stumbles and all that, but he can sit down and carry on a conversation. He can read, and he can write. There are rewards; there is a lot of joy.

People say to me, you don't have a TV set here, do you want us to give you a TV set for the house? I say: Why would we want a TV set? If you live at Annunciation House you don't need television. We have the most real-life *novela* here that one could want. Because people do not leave their feelings, their needs or desires or wants; they. don't leave them out on the streets when they come in here. They come totally as who they are.

Last November we had a wedding between a young woman from Guatemala and a young man from Nicaragua. That whole courtship happened here, and they got married here. It is impossible not to become attached. You cannot live with people and not become attached. If you can do that, I suggest that you go have an electrocardiogram done on you because there may be questions as to whether or not you are living. Maybe you need oxygen or something.

ARTISTS

The whole thing grew out of a strange confusion that I was never to resolve. A Mexican painter named Antonio Álvarez, who knew of my interest in the border, sent me a postcard from Puebla, saying that I should contact the poet Jorge Humberto Chávez in Juárez. There was a five-digit phone number. "I wish he'll give you information," wrote Antonio. "A big hug from Mexico."

One evening, after checking into a hotel in Juárez, I dialed the number for Jorge Humberto. At the name of Antonio Álvarez, the poet drew a total and complete blank. *"No le conozco—"* He didn't know him; he was certain, in fact, that they had never even met. However, he agreed to meet and talk about Juárez.

Later that night, Jorge Humberto Chávez arrived at the hotel. He was a slightly built young Mexican with a European flair. He wore a tailored double-breasted topcoat over a v-neck sweater and a long wool muffler in a style that reminded me of artists I had seen in Paris, Barcelona, Rome. His heavy black-framed glasses had tinted lenses that lent a look of seriousness to his thin face. He had with him a younger writer named Marco Antonio García Delgado, also a member of the Taller Literario de Ciudad Juárez, the Juárez Literary Workshop.

Like most of the Mexicans I have known, Jorge Humberto was forthcoming with his suggestions and generous with his time. Smoking one Marlboro after another, he called a few of the other writers and artists working in Juárez. It was decided that, the next evening, after he finished his teaching day, we would get together with other members of the workshop and begin looking at *their* Juárez. This promised to be different from anything I had seen of this city, which I had glimpsed fleetingly on my first Mexican trip, and which I had been visiting regularly for a number of years.

The following evening, Jorge showed up with Willivaldo Delgadillo, who was a fiction writer from the workshop and a well-known local

Miguel Angel Chavez Diaz de Leon, poet

activist. Willivaldo dressed in the kind of dark oversize clothes popular in the United States and Europe: full, pleated pants, shirt with large cargo pockets, corner rivets, extra plackets, and tabs.

Willivaldo was a *fronterizo* in the full sense of the word. He had learned to use the border like a tool. He had been born in Los Angeles; his mother had brought him to Juárez as a baby; he had lived here all of his life. Then, exercising his right as a U.S. citizen, he had attended high school in El Paso, though he continued to live in Juárez.

That much of his life remained unchanged. Each day he crossed the bridge into El Paso, where he worked as a paralegal, and then returned each night to the little house where he lived with his grandmother and a younger cousin. He was active in political movements on both sides of the river; he had sets of friends in Juárez and El Paso; he lived a kind of double life under the same set of convictions.

This style of living is not unusual on the border. Recent statistics have shown that at least 34,000 Juárenses cross into the U.S. legally in order to work. Some others are different from these daily commuters in that they do seasonal work in the U.S. and return to Mexico for extended periods. One of these was Sandra Sánchez. She was born in Eagle Pass, Texas, of Mexican parents. They all moved to Chicago, where she went to school. She has worked and traveled in a number of places in the States, but she prefers living in Mexico, where she has a house in Guadalupe Bravos below Juárez. She lives here, surrounded by many of her relatives, as much of the time as she can. "This is the life," she smiles. "You get money over there and bring it back here and live until it's finished."

They had brought me a copy of the magazine put out by the literary workshop. It was called *NOD*. The title had been inspired by the Book of

Genesis, by the same chapter from which John Steinbeck had taken the title *East of Eden*. The three pertinent verses appeared on the inside front cover:

> 13 Y dijo Caín a Jehová: Grande es
> mi castigo para ser soportado,
>   14 He aquí me echas hoy de la tierra,
> y de tu presencia me esconderé, y seré
> errante y extranjero en la tierra;
>   16 Salió, pues, Caín de delante de
> Jehová, y habitó en tierra de Nod, al
> oriente de Edén.

This quotation reflected more than simply the spirit of the magazine. In it was the spirit of the entire group of artists I was to meet. I would discover that, in their own way, they felt they were outcasts, strangers from Mexico, living in their own Nod, which was also called Juárez.

From the hotel, we swung onto Avenida de la Americas, squeezed into the rush-hour traffic on Avenida de 16 Septiembre, passing a string of mansions, including the one inhabited by the mayor of Juárez, and made our way slowly into the heart of the city. This land had been first explored by Fray Augustín Rodríguez and Antonio de Espejo in 1591, when it was called Paseo del Norte. The city itself came into existence almost seventy years later with the founding of Mission de Nuestra Señora de Guadalupe by Fray García de San Francisco. It had grown as a frontier outpost, a gateway to the important northern settlements in New Mexico.

Often on the streets in the cities of Mexico I have the feeling that the drivers feel they are competing in one big game of bumper cars. It seemed especially true that night as we passed the *mercado* and turned onto Avenida Lerdo. Cars made crazy turns, cutting across two or three lanes of traffic; they lurched ahead, ran lights, stopped for no reason. Someone once explained to me that they thought it was a problem of combining the machismo of the typical Mexican male with a lethal machine. Willivaldo said that here on the border it was far more fundamental; it was the result of the fact that people had money to buy cars, and they put them on the roads before they really knew how to handle them. It was the slapdash way the Third World operated. "What is it," he smiled, "putting the cart before the horse?"

We arrived at Plaza Cervantine, with its gold bust of the great Spanish writer and bas-relief representations of Don Quixote and Sancho Panza. Around this tiny plaza were buildings housing studios and living quarters for various artists and musicians. Jorge hammered on the door of the studio where Mario Arnal G. ran a workshop called Taller Libre de Experimentación Plástica, a workshop of the local experimental painters and sculptors. A woman leaned out an upstairs window and said he had already gone, look in the café.

Across the street we slipped into a grid of passageways at the base of a building and wound our way to El Coyote Invalido, an upbeat coffee shop where we found Mario at a table with three of the Juárez painters. It was here that these artists came to talk, discuss, and argue, a custom more European than American; I felt certain that across the river in El Paso I probably would not find a similar scene with the local artists.

We talked over a cup of good Mexican coffee, and I arranged to return to Plaza Cervantine the next morning to see the workshop. Willivaldo and Jorge asked about a certain theater director, but he seemed to have dropped out of sight that night.

Mario Arnal, Plaza Cervantine

Returning to the street, we walked around the corner to another café. It was a plain, cafeteria-style lunchroom with large windows, booths around the sides of the room, and tables in the middle.

"Look, there's Octavio."

"This is even better," said Willivaldo. "We were looking for a different guy, but I think Octavio is the best director in Juárez."

His name was Octavio Trias. With his curly hair and his boyish look, he reminded me of a poet I had known in London named Brian Patten. He had just finished eating with his wife and six-year-old son. The child was having a hard time staying awake through the last bites of a large bowl of ice cream. Octavio suggested we follow him home; they could get the child to bed, and then we could talk.

We drove south and east a few blocks and ended in a cul-de-sac at a small house tightly wedged between its neighbors. Then, while Octavio's wife undressed the sleeping child in the next room, I asked Octavio what had brought him to Juárez.

"Most of us get here by accident," he replied, scooting into the corner of a small couch to get comfortable. "We come here because we want to improve our living condition, our existence."

Octavio had moved to Juárez from Chihuahua, the capital of the state, a smaller, much calmer, and considerably more complacent city. The border, by contrast, was the place where a young person could get ahead; it held promise, possibility; even in these bad times, money could be made.

Juárez had not been an easy place for the theater, either to see it or to make it happen. "Although Chihuahua is a more conservative and closed city than Juárez," he said, "the theater adventure there has gone further in terms of form. The theater here is far behind."

He paused and laughed. "Don't get me wrong. By my arriving in Juárez the theater here was not saved."

That he might be misunderstood was not new to Octavio. "I have always been very progressive about my work. I like to do things that are different and experimental. That kind of theater is not without its problems anywhere. But here the people sometimes really freak out."

"Is there a border theater?"

"There is a Chicano theater," he said. He had worked with some of those plays. But what he was attempting to do was very different from conventional drama.

"We are doing what we call *invisible* theater." He was easier now, more excited to be talking. "These are small skits that we perform at a bus station, in the market, or other places where there are a lot of people. They are only skits, but people don't often realize that. They think it is for real. We work like the Living Theater. We create a situation that is real, and we get their attention in that way."

"What do you mean by *real* situations?"

"Okay, here in Juárez some of the girls who work in the *maquiladoras* have pimps. They are not prostitutes, but they still have pimps, or what amount to pimps. These guys never marry them. They get them pregnant, they have kids with them, but they don't marry them. They're like pimps. They make sure the girls go to work, then they go to the plants on Fridays, when the girls get paid, take them to cash their paychecks, and take the money from them."

Willivaldo spoke up: "It's a big problem here. So much of the work created by the *maquiladoras* is only for women. And you've got these guys trying to figure out how to get it."

"Right now," Octavio said, "we are working on this skit where a couple get into a fight because she doesn't want to give the guy her check anymore. They keep fighting and a lot of other things come out. The woman says she's tired of being mistreated, tired of him taking her money and running around."

"Does anyone recognize that it is theater?"

"No. So far, nobody has realized that we are performing a skit. They think it's a real fight by real people."

Octavio has no illusions that theater is so effective it can bring about sweeping cultural changes. But he sees this kind of street theater as at least having some positive results. "We know that we are not going instantly to revolutionize either the theater or the women to whom we want to send this message. But if fifty women are watching the skit, which they think is a fight, at least two of them are probably going through the same situation, and they are going to gain some awareness and, hopefully, do something about it."

Octavio admits that, in terms of professional satisfaction, these bits of *invisible* theater must be measured in a different way. "In one sense it is very fulfilling because you go directly to the people and you see the power of theater. But from the standpoint of conventional professional theater, it isn't very fulfilling because there is no applause, no real recognition of your work. Then, too, there is some danger. We have had people pushed around by the crowd. People throw things. Last time we had to finish sooner than usual because the police showed up."

Jorge Humberto Chávez lived on another quiet street not far from Octavio's. When we arrived at his house, we found other members of the *taller literario* waiting for us—Rosario Sanmiguel, Marco Antonio Garciá Delgado, Miguel Angel Chávez Díaz de León. They had been killing time with a Pac-Man game on the TV screen. I shook their hands, and then Jorge Humberto drew me aside into a dark room. He wanted me to see his *hijos*, his children.

Soft doorlight slicing across the floor gave just enough illumination to make out the children's features. He brushed hair away from the little girl's face and tucked the blankets up over the bodies of the two little boys. He told me how much he loved them. It was a touching moment, one I would remember later when I read his poem about his wife, *"Rosa Isela Ramírez, mi mujer—"*

Unlike Octavio, Jorge was a true *Juárense.* He had been born in Juárez. "I am from here," he declared. "All my family is here. This is my place. I have not consciously made the decision to live here. I just do. I belong to this city."

Was there some reason why he thought he should stay?

"I stay because there is a lot of work to be done," he said simply. "My work can be divided in two. On the one hand there is my work as a writer. On the other hand there is my work as a cultural promoter, helping to pro-mote magazines or theater or things that are aimed at opening alternatives for people who don't have that many choices."

We were crowded into his study. For him to have this room in such a small house was an obvious sacrifice for his family. His books were neatly arranged on shelves; his gleaming IBM typewriter, which seemed like the biggest thing in the room, stood on his desk; and above the desk was a

Jorge Humberto Chavez and family

Jorge Humberto Chavez, poet

sheet of cork to which were pinned messages, notes, addresses, cartoons. In his room, he had suddenly become very serious. "This city is full of life. Life here is very intense. That is why I have never been tempted to move to the interior—because there the life is much slower. I think maybe this is a romantic notion, but I would like to stay here and help realize some cultural manifestations that are not so well organized. I'd like to help improve their quality."

"Do you think your efforts can help change Mexico?"

Jorge Humberto pondered the question. "I don't know. I don't think about changing Mexico. I only hope I can reach certain people and change some of their attitudes."

"I do think about changing Mexico," said Rosario Sanmiguel, a writer of very powerful short fiction and the only woman in the *taller literario*. "But I think that any cultural manifestation can elevate levels of consciousness and sensibility and that through this the change will come."

Rosario had been born in a tiny border town in Coahuila, and, like Willivaldo, she had been brought here as a baby. Her father was a successful customs broker, dealing in spices and other export goods going

Rosario Sanmiguel, writer

into the U.S. Still, she didn't have the same kind of attachment to Juárez that Jorge Humberto had. She said she would leave. In the past she had lived and worked in Mexico City. "If I left again, I would still do the same kind of writing I'm doing now—because it comes out of my cultural background, out of the things I know."

But right now she was satisfied being in Juárez. Like Willivaldo, she crossed into El Paso each day. She taught Spanish in a junior college there, a job that had broadened her perspective on the border. Its themes were the themes of her stories. She recognized the violence and other forces that have brought enormous change to the area. "We feel those things here," she said. "There are a lot of people coming up from the rest of Mexico to cross the border. That brings a lot of pressure, and that has affected the life here—our lives and the way we think."

"What do you think about all the Mexicans leaving the country?"

"I think if people do not have what they need in their own place, they have the right to look for it wherever it is. If the government or the land can't give them the bread or salt that they need, they have the right to find it."

Jorge Humberto gave the argument a new turn: "Most of the artistic people," he said, "are not leaving the country. But we have a different problem. They are taking off from their provinces and going to Mexico City. They are clustering there."

"We stay here for that reason," said Rosario. "We are fighting against that centralism."

"It's true," Willivaldo agreed. He had begun to pace, taking short turns in the close room as he talked. "We have a strange sense of belonging. We feel that we belong and that we don't belong. We are from Juárez. We are aware that we are very special. We are very tied to the city and very much a part of it."

"What does it mean to be a part of a city that is in a state of constant change?"

"It is a different experience. From the outside it looks as if we have no culture here. But in Juárez there is a very intense cultural life." As Willivaldo spoke, all of the other young writers in the room were watching him and they were nodding him on. "Except our cultural life is not expressed in conventional ways. There are no plays every week, no weekly poetry readings; there aren't several literary journals published here. If a cultural anthropologist were to come to Juárez looking for documents that prove there is an intense cultural experience here, he would probably not find that evidence. You have to go out and walk the streets to find the culture. Octavio is doing street theater, religious people are at work, we have mural newspapers."

"But how is that so different from avant-garde culture in Mexico City?"

"The main difference is the place," Willivaldo said emphatically. "We are on the border. People from the United States come here all the time. And we cross over to El Paso. We see four channels of American television. Many of us know English. We have driven cabs, worked in bars, gone to school. Common people here can speak English. Many people feel that we have assimilated into the American culture, that we are not Mexicans anymore."

There was a murmur of agreement among the others.

"We are very cynical, though," Willivaldo went on. "We are not Americans, of course." (Willivaldo was a U.S. citizen, but the point he was making was philosophical.) "But we also don't care if we are Mexicans or not. We are different people in a different circumstance—people caught in an economic crisis."

They were Mexicans, but they had been forced to think of themselves as separate from Mexico. It was an outcry that I had heard and read about many times along the border. Sometime the previous year, I had clipped from a publication in Juárez an editorial opinion concerning the book *Distant Neighbors* by Alan Riding:

Leyendo el libro "Vecinos Distantes" de Alan Riding me encontre en el prólogo con un párrafo que dice así: Problmente en ningun lugar del mundo 2 paises son tan diferentes uno del otro y viviendo lado a lado.

Mas que por niveles de desarrollo, los 2 paises estan separados por el lenguaje, religión, raza, filosófia e história.

Creo que dicha apreciacion esta fundamentada en lo obvio, en un vistazo superficial. Creo que Sr. Riding nunce ha vivido en la frontera.

These young writers did live on the *frontera*, the border. It had formed their lives, their thinking; its elements were in their blood.

For Rosario it was very clear-cut: "In certain ways with our work we are trying to recreate the atmosphere that is special to us in Juárez. The subjects we take on are usually universal—love, solitude, death, et cetera. But these themes are treated through the eyes of characters from the border. If we look at the history of Mexican literature we find that very little has been written about the north, the border."

"Yes," Willivaldo added. "And we find our characters here. Why did Rosario, for example, choose a prostitute who is dying in a hospital? In the story a man walks out of a hospital and takes a cab to downtown Juárez. He goes to a bar and starts talking to the owner, but he is thinking about his woman back in the hospital. He had been a showman in a bordello, and he and the whore had fallen in love. As he is about to leave, the madam comes over and says to tell Lucia that she still has her room here. Lucia and the man had tried to get away and live a conventional life. Now she is dying. And the madam is making fun of them. Because we live here those themes are real for Rosario. This is the life we see."

Finally, as far as really taking the basic themes of the border, all the writers from the *taller* felt that Miguel Angel Chávez Díaz de León, the younger brother of Jorge Humberto, used them in their simplest and most direct forms. Was this, I asked, a conscious decision on his part.

"No," Miguel Angel said, his brow furrowing. "Other people have asked the same question. I think it has to do with the fact that I grew up in a neighborhood here in Juárez. I write about my living experiences and the people I grew up with. I write about this collective experience, and I try to do it in a very simple language, not looking for stilted words or complicated structures. I try to do it in a fresh way."

Miguel Angel has never strayed very far from this life. With his wife, he manages and works in a fast-food place called Mex-Donalds. In this way, he stays close to the people whose lives, interacting with his own, form the thematic heart of his poems.

"The border itself," he confessed, "comes out in my poems because of a special experience I have with it."

"How do you mean, *special?*"

"I go to El Paso to buy the paper and supplies I use in making my poems. I do this illegally. I know it is illegal, but I do it for the experience. That has influenced the way I write my poems. I cross in a spot not far from the bridge. There is a tunnel that I go running through with only my shorts on." When he reaches the other side, he dresses and then goes to the office supply stores that stock the kind of paper, pens, and other things that he favors.

Behind the formal simplicity of his writing style is an acute cultural awareness shared in different ways by most of the members of the *taller*. It boils down to the basic things that make the border the border. And to Miguel Angel they meant this: "Here in Juárez there is a certain cultural and economic dependence on the United States that accentuates the fact that I want to feel Mexican. Because of the cultural shock that takes place on the border and the fact that Mexican culture is inferior to that of the United States, my experiences as a *fronterizo* are stronger."

There was a silence in the room. Willivaldo was first to express his dismay: "I can't believe he said that Mexican culture is inferior. We're all shocked. Always before he only spoke out against American culture."

Miguel Angel stood and left the room. The interview had ended.

In the days that followed I saw various sides of Juárez. It was an old city. In the 325 years since its founding it had grown to accommodate the changing border and the changing Mexico; for years it had indulged the passions of the United States and witnessed some of its tragedies. It was here, for example, that Ingrid Bergman had married Roberto Rosellini, that Frank Sinatra and Mia Farrow had been divorced, that Steve McQueen had died. Tourists came to play the horses, the dogs, and to watch the bulls be killed.

That was a plus, a boost for the economy. The problems were coming mostly out of the south. Now it was almost impossible to find living space. Since the earthquake, people had fled Mexico City to live here or to try and slip across into the United States. Their numbers had swelled the old barrios and the new developments. There was a floating population outside the official census that some people estimated to be in the hundreds of thousands. With it had come a devastating increase in crime and poverty, added burdens for a city trying to survive.

Juárez

With the aid of the *taller literario* group, I was able to move through various areas of Juárez, seeing aspects of the typical life of the town—barbers, funeral directors, coffin makers, *tortillerias*, people in the trades.

In the painter's workshop, Taller Libre de Experimentacion Plástica, in Plaza Cervantine, I was shown the art of Mario Arnal, Enrique Ramírez Martínez, Alfredo Tellez "Bandido," and others. It was a side of a Mexican border town that most people neither see nor suspect even exists.

After we left the workshop and were outside in the plaza again, Jorge Humberto began shouting: "Anzaldo! Anzaldo!"

The artist Manuel Anzaldo Menéses appeared on the highest balcony. He came down and unlocked the door. We ascended a narrow, very steep staircase to the top of the building, having to duck constantly because the doors were short and the ceiling was low. On the floor before his studio, a musician had been awakened by Jorge Humberto's shouting.

"Que pasa?" he grumbled.

I said: "We came to see Anzaldo."

Manuel Anzaldo Meneses, painter

"What do you want with that crazy asshole?" he moaned and covered his head with a blanket. We continued up to the small room that doubled as kitchen and studio. Back in the small bedroom, a baby slept beneath Anzaldo's painting of its mother.

Someone said Anzaldo had come from Mexico City. That would explain his more cosmopolitan look and life-style. He was bohemian in his dress, a layering of shirts and scarves that might in part have been influenced by his wife, a fabric designer. His wispy beard and mustache and the small collection of earrings he wore set him apart from the other artists I had seen that day.

"I can take you to see the whorehouses," he offered, his eyes lighting up. "The pleasure domes," he added in English, alluding to Coleridge.

He suggested I see the young girls who'd been lured or forced to come to the border and work as prostitutes. And I ought to see the gay clubs, the crazy places. He knew three or four that were typical. Rosario was still with us. I wondered how this would work out, until I recalled Willivaldo's description of one of her stories. It was all the border, their territory.

Walking along in front of us, his plastic "jelly bean" sandals clacking, Anzaldo was like a pied piper. He led the way into streets in the shadow of the cathedral. We ducked into a gay bar, which, except for the music, might have been in Greenwich Village. We went on to one where the stripper was a transsexual, an exotic "girl" from the U.S. She had a very sexy body, except her breasts seemed to have been set just a little too close together. A man nudged me. "You think she's something, man. I got the best buns you ever saw."

The third club was noisy and already crowded. It seemed that the same song was playing.

"This one," Anzaldo said at the door, "has older ladies."

"Older" put them somewhere in their early twenties. We took a large table next to the runway where the girls danced. One dancer, a statuesque girl with sturdy thighs and a very prominent ass, moved back and forth along the runway, swaying on her high heels. Gradually, through the next two songs, she stripped down to her panties. At the beginning of the third song she slipped off the black panties, putting them safely out of the reach of the customers, and began a serious search for action. Of the three or four men in the audience, one was watching with the kind of attention that told you his mouth had gone dry. The girl came down the runway to where Rosario sat, got down on her back, and scooted around in rhythm to the beat until her bush was almost in Rosario's face. The whore started to laugh and moved away to finish the song for the men.

The last club was larger, a cavernous place hung with the kind of colored ropes people put up at Christmas, and the ceiling was studded with strobe lights that flashed to the music. Anzaldo found the pimp. He was small, well-dressed, and wore a number of gold chains around his neck. Anzaldo introduced us and asked if I could go in the back and talk to the girls. It was obviously not a normal question. The pimp talked it over with the owner who was behind the bar watching a miniature TV. Anzaldo went over to the two of them. He was amazing. I thought he was going to climb over the bar to convince the owner I should be allowed back in the rooms.

Something worked. Anzaldo returned, smiling.

The door behind the dance floor led to a long corridor with rooms opening off of it. There was a huge woman in white sitting at a table with towels. She wore rollers in her hair and continued to crochet a pair of booties while we were led past.

I waited in one of the rooms, which had walls of cheap paneling, a double bed with nothing covering it except a flowered mattress pad. There was a bedside table and a tiny light bulb in the ceiling.

The girls were brought in and introduced. They were young, in their early teens, with the exception of two who seemed to be fully sixteen. One

*Transsexual
entertainer,
Juárez*

Juárez   pointed out that she was pregnant. She stood and asked if it showed. The pimp reached and stroked the bulge on her stomach and then kissed her. One of the older ones began to tease me. "Hey, gringo, stay for the night. I love what you've got between your legs."

The pimp began wrestling playfully with two of the girls on the bed. He was like a teddy bear to them. Suddenly there was a call for one of the girls, the youngest. The pimp sent her out. And it was time for us to leave. The man coming down the corridor looked a little confused, seeing us all emerging from the one room, and he turned to watch as we filed back into the smoky club and into the street.

The next morning was slow. By ten the sun had reached the hotel pool, and three Mexican girls had decided to brave the cold water. A group of young bankers here for a few days of seminars paused outside the coffee shop to compare notes. The attention of the bankers kept drifting to the girls. The girls knew it, of course. They were giggling and playing for the attention. Then the sleekest of the three climbed out of the pool and stepped onto the diving board. Immediately the poolside area became quiet. The young bankers in their three-piece suits moved toward the pool. The girl, acting as though nothing were happening, took a long time getting poised for her dive. Finally, she splashed into the water with no particular grace. The young bankers waited until she surfaced and then applauded.

I thought about the prostitutes I had seen the night before (some of the young bankers may have seen them as well). It was only fate, the hard fate of Mexico, that kept them out of the pool here, that made their lives different and their applause different, too.

Sunday I was to meet with the fiction writers, at their weekly workshop. Willivaldo was late picking me up. He had bought a car the day before in El Paso, and the battery had given out in the night. He and a friend had found another battery and got the car going. It was an aging four-door Pontiac with loose steering and a tricky automatic transmission that took a couple of seconds to engage. But it was big and it hadn't cost much, so Willivaldo bullied it through the streets of Juárez.

The meeting was at the house of Rosario Sanmiguel. The day before she had moved into a bungalow in a development located east of the Casas Grande Highway. The rooms were still piled up with boxes. Paintings leaned against the walls, and the furniture had been shoved into corners. One of the small bedrooms had been cleared. Her desk was set up, and there was a table surrounded by straight-back chairs. In the center were a few bottles of Coca-Cola.

The story that afternoon was Willivaldo's. It was a terse, carefully written, almost Hemingwayesque story. He read it for the group, stopping once to open a Coke, and the other four members of the *taller* were quick to get into their questions and criticisms. There was praise for certain of Willivaldo's strong imagery, doubt about aspects of one character, questions about the vague ending—not that it lacked resolution but that the resolution, strong as it was, was vague. In this small, plain room full of so much hope, so much promise, I could see the process at work. There was enthusiasm and passion in both the attack and the defense. The story would grow from it; so would the writer and his critics.

From Rosario's we made our way back to the center of the city, to the plaza in front of Our Lady of Guadalupe, the ancient mission started in 1659. It was dark. The Committee of Mothers of the Disappeareds had gathered to show a video tape for their cause, which was a vigilance for information concerning the sons they claimed had been taken by the Mexican police. A small Datsun pickup had been driven up to the steps with a large-screen TV console. A taped interview with one of the mothers was played for a silent crowd that continually grew. A banner had been hung with grainy black-and-white posters of the young men who had been taken. They were young faces, not unlike faces I'd seen around the table at Rosario's, in the studios and workshops.

One of the mothers said to me, her words echoing what I had been told so long ago before my first trip to the border: "This, too, is the border, señor, this is Mexico. *Tenga cuidado!* Be careful!"

"Derecho,"
Juárez city
dump

Marco Antonio
Garcia Delgado

*Man in
tortilleria,
Juárez*

*Street stand,
Juárez*

*Tortilleria,
Juárez*

*José Guadalupe
Diaz in his
studio*

Waiting out the rain, Juarez

Norteños, Bluetown, Texas

Near El Paso, Texas

TEACHERS

A slow cold rain in El Paso, a shroud of late winter clouds over Sierra de Cristo Rey and the Franklin Mountains, wind beginning to blow out of the south. Then, a hundred miles east, a brief peppering of icy hail danced off the highway between Sierra Blanca and Van Horn. The low cloud cover continued to Valentine and Marfa, but it was dry—a condition that had prevailed for most of the winter. In the hills near Shaftner a coyote trotted along the fence line, oblivious of my slowing car. Like beggars at a banquet, a group of black buzzards flapped and fought to rip flesh from the carcass of a car-struck deer. By the time I had dropped off the rimrock and started zigzagging down into Presidio, the sky had cleared and the afternoon was hot and still.

Farm Road 170 swung west past the Border Patrol facility and went roller-coasting along between the base of the hills and the Rio Grande, which many of the Mexicans in these parts still call Rio Bravo, the wild river. On the other side, in Mexico, a haze of dust hung over the streets of Ojinaga. Signs warned of flash flooding, and flood gauges stood in the beds of the arroyos. The road jogged south to miss the crumbling adobe church in Ruidosa and continued on to Candelaria, where the pavement came abruptly to an end. The explanation was that there was no state maintainance beyond that point, though there was a road of sorts.

It was here in Candelaria that I met Johnnie Chambers. With Tip Chesney, Johnnie teaches in a tiny white two-room schoolhouse flanked by two outdoor toilets and a playground, and situated between the church and the cemetery on a hill overlooking the village. She is a tall woman, with red hair that she keeps pulled back and up into a kind of severe twist on the top of her head. To find her suddenly peering down from the step above the porch, as I had that day, her large glasses reflecting the hard border sun, her hair ablaze, was enough to make me take a step back. She said if I would come at 2:30, we could talk during recess.

El Paso, Texas

Our conversation took place in the teacherage, where Johnnie was free to have a cigarette and a cup of instant tea, a drink she said she prefers to "real" tea. These two small rooms were her home five nights a week. They were cluttered with the work that spilled over from the school—books, papers she was reading and grading.

Johnnie had come down to the border to live when she married a rancher named Boyd Chambers. Raising a family in this remote place had been complicated—mostly because of school for her children. She moved back and forth between the ranch and Alpine or Presidio so the kids could get a decent education. She ran a soda fountain and did a few other things to make it all work. And maybe this had something to do with her decision to teach. At any rate, when her youngest son was three, she went back to college and got her teaching certificate. As she put it: "I always wanted six kids, but I had only four. My husband says I started teaching so I could have a whole bunch of kids, and I guess that's true. I've got hundreds and hundreds of kids."

There was a point she wanted to stress: "This is no ordinary school, you understand. My daughter-in-law does teach in one, though, and she, along with everyone else I know who teaches only one grade, is always saying, 'I can't stand that Ortega kid or that Williams kid. I'll be so glad when he goes into Mrs. Smith's class next year.' Well, it's different here. If you don't like a child in this school you'd better find something redeemable about him and *learn* to like him, because you're going to have to put up with that kid for the better part of about ten years. But," she added with a smile, "I don't guess there's a child that I don't like."

I asked if she had chosen Candelaria because the school was convenient to the ranch.

"No. I never intended to work here. What I wanted to teach was high school. But it seemed that so many of the teachers they had here just didn't care."

The same thing could never be said about Johnnie. She did care, and her teaching had gradually become more a calling than a job. "I've been teaching here and at Ruidosa for fourteen years, and I've just never been able to leave."

Part of the reason was the school, of course, but part of it was the place—the wild border country along the Rio Grande. "I do love it," she said, lighting a second cigarette. "Boyd, my husband, jokes about it. He says he never worries about me leaving him, because I might get mad at him but I'd never leave the country. I guess that's right. I know these people are sure different. You never just move in here and become one of the locals. You are accepted, and they are good to you. I mean, they are the most friendly people in the world, but outsiders are never quite one of them. Fifty years later, they'll still be saying, 'Oh, him—he's the fellow that moved down here from Dallas.' "

If she were in Houston or Austin or just about anyplace else in Texas, Johnnie would think nothing of a ten-mile commute to work. But here at

**Johnnie
Chambers in
the teacherage**

this border outpost a different set of rules applies to almost everything. "I live only about ten miles up in the Sierra Vieja mountains. That really doesn't seem very far until you've driven the road. But I come in on Sunday evening and stay until Friday afternoon. It's just too much trouble to get everything done here and try to drive back in the dark. This time of the year it can be dangerous to go home because I have to cross the creek five times between here and the ranch. There are no bridges, so if it rains you may make it and you may not. Get stuck and you have a choice: you either walk this direction or that direction. And at that time of evening I'm not really up to walking six or seven miles."

In fact, almost nothing that was standard procedure in the rest of America's schools seemed right for this border settlement. The school was bilingual, but only out of necessity. These were students from Mexican-American families; their first language had been Spanish, the language of their parents. "We don't teach in Spanish, though," Johnnie said. "We explain in Spanish anything that needs to be explained. But the parents are very adamant about English. They say their kids get Spanish at home, that they send them to school to learn English. And I agree. I think my main function is to teach them to speak English so they can function in the United States away from the border."

And she was determined to give all the time and attention it took to

Candelaria school

Presidio, Texas

accomplish that. "We start at eight and we don't let out until four."

Tip Chesney had come in to fix himself a cup of coffee. He was a young man, lean and fit, reminding me more of a camp counselor than a school teacher. He had been leaning against the counter, listening to Johnnie, waiting for the water to boil. Now he added: "We keep the ones that need extra work until four-thirty or five."

"Do they have any idea how lucky they are to have this kind of dedicated teachers?" I asked.

"I think they do appreciate it. Of course, they don't know that other teachers are different. They've never had any others. But they do find out how much they know that other kids don't know when we get kids from other schools. We had an Anglo come here from Ohio. He was the only Anglo I've ever taught besides my own son. The kids weren't too kind to him to start with. Then they found out how dumb he was. And, you know, everybody huddled around that kid and tried to help him. They thought it was just great that they were smarter than this gringo from the city."

Johnnie's day in school ends only when she runs out of hours. And her dedication seems to have been contagious. The kids don't let the bell govern their curiosity or their chance to learn. "Lots of times," Johnnie explained, "if they have a math problem or something they can't work out at home, they bring it back up to school. This teacherage is my office after school. They come with their books and we help them with whatever problems they have. We're just available, you might say, twenty-four hours a day."

Much of Johnnie's time has been spent working well beyond the requirements of her contract. Enthusiastic, generous, she reaches out, trying to leave her mark, trying to make her little part of the world, which she understands in a way few people could, a better place. Her ideas about education and her efforts to realize them have not been restricted by the international boundary that is clearly visible from the front door of the school. "I'm teaching an adult class in the late afternoons or evenings or whatever time it happens to be," she confessed. "I teach English to the young doctors and teachers and nurses from across the river in Mexico. And, bless their hearts, they wade knee-deep water to get here for classes. Now anybody that wants to learn that bad I can spend an hour or two hours a day trying to help them."

I stayed that afternoon and met some of the Mexican students. Her class was a lesson in foreign policy that might well have helped reduce our ridiculous arms expenditures and maybe even cut our collective paranoia about the surge of communism through our southern border. (I learned a few months later that one of the male students I'd met that day had been brutally murdered in some kind of squabble that was related to problems peculiar to the border. He had apparently been dragged behind a pickup and left for dead. An autopsy revealed that he had lived for nine days and, although both legs were broken, he had dragged himself a number of miles trying to find help.)

*Three of
Johnnie's
students from
Mexico*

Tip Chesney

Tip and Johnnie at school, Candelaria, Texas

One big problem at the Candelaria School has always been convincing the students that they should go on to high school after they have finished the eighth grade. As recently as a year ago the problem was compounded by the lack of bus service to and from the high school in Presidio. Then the road was paved, and it was possible to get a bus up to them. "The girls we have going to high school were six weeks late last year because we were waiting for the road to be finished. Then we still couldn't get the school district to send the bus. We drove them down for a few weeks. Finally, Presidio started sending a bus. Legally, I think they had to do it, but they weren't going to actually make the effort until they were forced to."

As could be expected, Johnnie Chambers has been relentless in her fight to bring high school education to her pupils. She has never confined herself simply to standing in front of her class, admonishing them with a stern finger, and warning them of the consequences of failing to get a diploma. "I do go to great lengths to try and get them in high school," she said, standing up and taking her empty cup to the sink. "I had a girl leave here and go over to Pecos. I found out that she wasn't in school, that instead of going on to high school she had taken a job at one of the motels, cleaning rooms. So, just before high school started, I went to visit her immediate superior. I told her that this was a schoolgirl who needed to continue her education. She said she would make arrangements for her to work after school. Then I sent word up by one of her cousins that I was going to check and make sure she was going to school. If she wasn't in school, I threatened to bring my paddle. She told the cousin that she was going to school. She would be too embarrassed if I showed up at the motel with my paddle."

Johnnie laughed. "And she did go. She finished high school."

Johnnie was proud of that. I saw it flash in her eyes. "You have these kids so many years. Sometimes I take them when they're four and have them through the eighth grade. That's ten years, if they don't fail. It's kind of like your own kids. You don't have them much longer than that. And you don't see them near as much during the day. You have a particular fondness for each one of these kids, and you get to know them very well. You push them, you try to help them develop. We have one boy in the fifth grade who is already doing eighth-grade math, reading, and language. Now we've got him working on the computer. We've had a couple like him— bright, bright kids capable of anything."

There were others who had also benefited from Johnnie Chambers's unusual methods of teaching. If sometimes the approach was unorthodox, the result more than made up for it. "I have a little thing I do if I find out some kid isn't going to go to high school. I fail him. It's just a matter of course. That way they're going to get one more year. We never teach them the same things. We just extend their education."

She started clearing away the tea cups. It was time to get back to class.

A few months later, Johnnie Chambers invited me to the ranch for their annual butchering. Over the phone she said it probably sounded strange and admitted that it probably was. But, for some reason, people just turned up year after year. To a lot of the friends of this unusual family, it had become a traditional get-together, a party on the border.

The road to the ranch continued where the pavement left off in Candelaria and the track became a bed of loose cobbles. "Keep going down a long grade to where the road forks at the creek," Johnnie had said. "Take the right turn across the creek (you're going to cross the creek five times), then keep to the main road. Cross a cattle guard and keep going to the first aluminum gate. At the second aluminum gate turn left back across the creek. You are less than two miles from the house at this point, so just keep coming."

I could appreciate Johnnie's not wanting to drive this road on a rainy night. Even in this dry time, the creek ran enough water to send steam up from the manifold and muffler and make me slip into four-wheel drive to climb up the opposite banks. What Johnnie had not mentioned over the phone was how, once you passed Candelaria and started back into the Sierra Vieja Mountains, the country was suddenly more beautiful. The first spring foliage of the mesquite was a soft shade of light green. There was candelia, a plant once useful for its wax; there were endless creosote bushes, sotol, and yucca. The first of the spring flowers were out—yellow and blue.

The road swung sharply up a hill, crested, and from the top the house was visible. Square and fortresslike, put up with stones and mortar in a country where adobe is more common, it looked just slightly out of place. There were water tanks on the high rocks behind it and corrals and out-buildings to the north. It was said that the house had been built in 1911 by a member of the Burroughs family associated with the famous Burroughs Corporation, as a retreat for an alcoholic son. There was, in fact, in one building adjacent to the house a room fitted with barred windows. To that family, this ranch on the Rio Grande, in the exact middle of nowhere, was the perfect spot to isolate their son from booze.

What they had overlooked was that across the river was the state of Chihuahua, notorious for its bootlegging into the U.S. Specifically, there was the town of Coyame, noted for its sotol. Sotol is a colorless but highly potent liquor distilled from the sotol plant and bears on its label (which has only recently been pasted onto any bottles I've seen) the warning that its consumption can be harmful to your health, causing nausea and vomiting. At any rate, Mexicans who had worked on the ranch in those early days told stories of vast quantities of sotol stored in the high cupboards of the kitchen. Maybe it was the overriding spirit of those past times, together with the mystery of not ever being able to learn what had become of poor Burroughs, that was to turn this into a maverick weekend.

The yard was already jammed with four-wheel-drive vehicles belonging to the odd collection of people who'd come to help Johnnie and Boyd Chambers do their yearly butchering. As I made my way to the house, I shook hands with a few of them. There was Marlowe, the mailman who made the trip down from Marfa during the week to bring mail to this area. There was a nurse with her dachshund. There were teachers, a librarian, a writer working on the *Handbook of Texas*, a medical technician, a surplus dealer, a storekeeper, the owners of a hot springs

spa, a sheriff, a biologist and a wetback—only one and he, like the rest of us, was a guest. More people were expected and would continue to drag in until the early hours of the morning.

I found Johnnie in the kitchen. She was wearing a funny green sun hat and demonstrating to a group of women the proper way to add hard-boiled eggs to a potato salad. She had been prompted to do this when she had seen one of the women take a knife to an egg and start cutting it into the kind of slices you might see as garnish in a delicatessen. Johnnie's method was different. "You separate the white from the yolk. You break the white into small pieces. Then you smush the yolk and add it sort of like crumbs."

"Smush?" questioned an English teacher. "How the hell do you conjugate *smush*?"

Johnnie laughed, but she was clearly out of sorts over something

Boyd Chambers cutting meat, annual butchering, Chambers Ranch

more important than hard-boiled eggs. The cause, I found, was a statewide teacher's competency test she had been forced to take the previous Monday. It was a major bone of contention between Texas teachers and Governor White and the Texas legislature. Some of the teachers had just shrugged it off. But the test had not set well with Johnnie. She objected to many of the questions, she thought the essay question was stupid, and she hated the whole idea.

Boyd Chambers chuckled about it from the stove where, with his rolled-brim cowboy hat pushed back, he put the finishing touches on a huge pot of "son-of-a-gun" stew, which bubbled and sputtered over the burner. "This is one discussion I plan to stay plumb out of," he said.

The wetback came in with another big pot for Boyd and was introduced as Lupe, Guadalupe Lopez. Boyd gave him a beer and sent him down to start a fire in one of the barbeque pits. Lupe, Boyd explained, didn't work on the ranch; he had a job on another ranch somewhere to the north. But each spring on his way to Mexico he always stopped. Like the others, Lupe just showed up. He wasn't hired to help, but he did help. And, in Boyd's words, "He can damn sure outwork any two Mexicans I've ever seen."

Boyd had already begun creating barbecue sauce for the next day. He was dumping the contents of whole cans and bottles into the huge pot.

Someone asked his recipe. "Damned if I know," he said. "I just use whatever I can find up there in the cupboard." But watching him revealed a somewhat less cavalier attitude toward his selection of ingredients. And the results, when we tasted the *cabrito* cooked in his sauce the next afternoon, would certainly be proof of his skill.

Partly, I think, to get herself out of the teachers' conversation, Johnnie took me on a tour of the house. It was old and substantial, with walls almost a yard thick. She had tiny cacti growing in pots and tins on the south porch. Among them were tightly budded peyotes and some that seemed to be growing hair. She had collected several thousand arrowheads and other Indian artifacts from various sites on the ranch. Some of these were arranged on velvet and framed. But most of them were in drawers or cans and boxes. If she had any time to spare, she used it to do something, to grow something, to study something. A stack of books had already collected for summer reading.

There is a certain kind of measuring that western men do, Texas men in particular. Out in the yard it was already beginning. One man had invited another to his truck to show him something. It was magnetic. Gradually a small group of men collected at the open door of the pickup while the owner reached into the glove compartment for his new pistol. Variations on this scene would be repeated throughout the day, with a slight change in details; the gun would be pulled from under a seat or maybe from the bottom of a suitcase. This one was a .38 Special in a leather holster. There would be a .357 Magnum still in the box, a .9 mm in a zipper case where it lay against red plush, a .45 automatic wrapped in a piece of soft leather. The onlookers would set their beer cans on the hood or roof of the vehicle and inspect the piece, weighing it carefully in their hands, taking aim at something in the distance, and then pass it on. They handled each unfamiliar gun the way men handle someone else's baby or a rare jewel.

Later these firearms were strapped on, and a shooting expedition was organized. Three carloads of people drove out of the yard just before sundown, the dust from their tires turning bright orange as it rose behind them. Then after a few minutes we heard the reports of the heavy-caliber ammunition echoing back from a canyon.

Boyd looked up from his barbecue sauce to which he had just added the final ingredient, tabasco sauce, and declared in his slow voice: "Well, I guess they finally drank enough beer to believe they were rich enough to afford to burn up that kind of ammunition."

*Teresa Baeza and
her children with a
friend from Mexico,
Candelaria, Texas*

The teachers in the kitchen were still lamenting their test, bringing Governor White closer to a public tar and feathering. The sun had set, and to the west the sky had already run through half a dozen colors. The air had cooled with the colors of the sky.

I walked down to where Lupe was busy tending the fire. He was sixty-seven years old, short, his wide features and strong wiry body evidence of his Indian heritage. That night he wore a polyester leisure suit and a pair of running shoes with Velcro closings. He had worked over here for *veinte cuatro años*, twenty-four years. Most of those years had been on the same ranch, though he had been many places—New Mexico, Utah, Idaho, Montana, Wyoming, Colorado, Nebraska. He said he'd never had trouble with Immigration. He had been careful and smart—at this point, he touched a finger to his temple. And he had never pressed his luck. Luck, *suerte* in Spanish, where the word is used more frequently and with more seriousness than in English, was everything to Lupe.

Someone making a beer run to the cooler in the back of a Jeep asked Lupe if he wanted another *cerveza*.

"*Si, como no?*" he replied, finishing off the one in his hand and tossing it into a trash barrel.

In all his years of living in the United States, Lupe had not learned to speak English. He understood it well. But he preferred Spanish. And, anyway, English was not necessary to his job. He had had almost no formal education, but life had taught him many lessons about the heart and the soul—*corazón y alma*. He indicated how his heart beat. He had enjoyed life. And he continued to make it enjoyable. He spoke of a whorehouse where he still went to take a room, and a woman, for a night—not an hour or half an hour.

From the back of the house the dinner bell sounded. Son-of-a-gun (or "the gentleman from Alpine," as Boyd was now calling it), beans, tortillas, potato salad, tamales, biscuits, vegetables, dips, and numerous desserts filled the table, stove, and counter of the kitchen.

"We always worry about not having enough," Johnnie said, watching her guests fill their plates and find a place to sit and eat. "But I don't think anybody ever went hungry at one of these things yet."

It was after dinner, with the night cold coming fast with sundown and everyone gravitating toward the hot mesquite fire down in the yard, that the first bottle of sotol appeared. Most of the people who had sampled it over the years had never seen a bottle bearing a label. The stuff was tested with caution. Jokes were made about the warning on the label, though nobody doubted its veracity. Lupe took turns with Tip, the teacher, and his friend Glen. The bottle circulated. There were a few takers on the first round, but that number dwindled significantly with each subsequent round. Most people stuck to beer.

The sotol had a flavor peculiar to liquors distilled from the cacti of Mexico. It was smooth enough at first, but it had a bite and a kick and a

*Lupe
(Guadalupe
Lopez)*

seductive warmth that seemed to start and build. It wasn't exactly friendly. You could tell that after the first few drinks.

Marlowe, the mailman, waved the bottle on. The man standing next to him took a shot and, with a shake of his head, said, "This's the damnedest shit I ever drank. One minute you're up and talking, and the next minute it's just like somebody hit you with a two-by-four. You're flat on your back, and somebody's taking your pulse to see if you're even alive."

Glen, the writer for the *Handbook of Texas*, remembered a dream he had had after a particular sotol drunk. He and Tip Chesney had taken a quart jar of sotol down to the banks of the Rio Grande near Candelaria. They had built a fire and shared the bottle, drinking and talking until they both finally passed out. Glen was awakened by some troops of Pancho Villa. They said Villa wanted to meet him. They insisted that he hurry, that Villa was waiting and growing impatient. Glen tried to wake Tip, but Tip had passed out so bad there was no way to get a move out of him. And when Glen turned to go by himself the troops had left. He woke hours later, the morning sun burning hot on his face and already adding to his misery. The dream was still so vivid that he jumped up and, despite his throbbing head, tried to find hoof prints the Villistas' horses would have left in the sand on the river bank.

In the ensuing silence, while the story thinned out into the night, I recalled a photograph I had seen somewhere of Pancho Villa waiting in a grove of trees in Coahuila. It was July 1920, and he was with, I believe, General Felipe Angeles. Both are smoking. Pancho Villa cups his cigarette in his palm between thumb and forefinger, the way workmen and peasants often smoke. His big straw is on one of his knees and his knotlike bare head gives a look of real power to his muscular body. I could understand Glen's dream. I, too, would love to have met Pancho Villa.

Talk turned to Halley's Comet; I was the only one who had seen it—an unconvincing blur in the evening sky the previous November. Here on the ranch, at the edge of nowhere, the sky was crystal clear and the time was perfect for an early-morning sighting. Plans were made either to set an alarm for 4:30 or to stay up. Someone had seen a story in a Mexican magazine that linked the appearance of the comet with the disaster of the *Challenger* space shuttle. This brought more silence than laughter. Johnnie stood up and announced that she was going to bed, adding that there was a lot of butchering to do in the morning. A statement that brought everything back to earth.

By eleven o'clock it had grown very cold. Lupe kept the mesquite fire stoked with big logs. People stood as close as they could and turned frequently to warm their cold side. At one point, Tip reached out and poured a few drops of sotol on the coals. Flames shot up. Someone said mescal would do the same thing. One of the women said the worm in the bottle of mescal was too much for her; *Gusano Rojo*, she gagged everytime she tried to drink it. Someone else remembered a liquor from Vietnam or Korea that contained the remains of a poisonous snake. Tip contended that none of it could hold a candle to sotol. He saluted with the second bottle and then set it close to the coals so it would warm. He claimed that a little heat improved the taste.

The sotol had left Lupe a little soft on his feet. He said the word *snake*, using *víbora* in Spanish. Up in the Sierra Viejas he had killed a *víbora*. He made a circle in the air with the fingers of both hands to indicate its size; then he stepped off its length, at least three long steps. Fangs as long as his forefingers. And nubs growing from its head almost like horns. And when he measured it again it seemed to have grown. He leaned down and brought the sotol out of the fire. There was a warm glaze in his eyes as he took a long drink from the bottle.

Three months later, in Zapata, Texas, I saw on the wall of a cafe the framed skin and rattles of a snake at least as big as the one described by Lupe. The man at the cash register called it *abuelo*, grandfather; a woman cradling a baby muttered *diablo*, the devil.

With the final dark long after midnight came a silence punctuated only by outbursts of dreamlike talk that resembled confession or bits of lost memories. Once or twice coyotes could be heard, a triangular conversation from the hills to the east.

Everyone felt the need for music. A portable stereo set up on the hood of a Jeep pumped Jimmy Buffet's "Desperation Samba" out through its tiny speakers:

> I wonder how in the hell I got here
> Halloween in Tijuana
> Full moon in my eyes
> I wonder how in the hell I got here
> Without a disguise

I began talking with the biologist, who was from Sul Ross State University in Alpine. He had entered his profession, after a last failed marriage and a time of being desperate and lost, because he wanted something that would keep him in this country. The border in this part of Texas was strange. It was desolate, but it was a beautiful, rich desolation. The border bred people who never wanted to move away, and the region attracted others who, once they'd come here, found it hard to live in any other place.

The biologist spent months at a time down here, living out of his pickup, studying a few acres of the desert up a nearby canyon. The major thrust of his study had to do with a certain strain of pocket mice. There were technical connections he was making between these particular mice and a similar mouse in Mexico. Occasionally he lost me in a sea of scientific jargon. But we shared a mutual respect for this kind of desert and an amazement for the abundance of life that it supported.

And Jimmy Buffet helped: *"Yo quiero a bailar en Mexico—"* Of course, the biologist's point about the border needed no proof that could not be found there at the edge of that fire. The people who had gathered and were now backing away, stumbling toward their beds to sleep off the load of a long day's drinking, had been drawn here for reasons that went beyond the desire to help the Chambers family fill their freezer with meat.

Boyd was up early, long before sunrise—though he didn't bother with the comet. Marlowe, the mailman, sat in the kitchen with him, trying to coax his feet into a pair of scuffed roper boots while he waited for the cowboy coffee to boil and the grounds to settle. Lupe, who could not have had more than a couple of hours' sleep, was already reviving the fire. It would be, he said, rubbing his wrinkled brow, a beautiful day. Not too hot, no clouds, no wind. There could be no wind with the moon we had had. He took a short pull on the sotol.

"No mucho," he said in Spanish, "just a little for the stomach."

No one looked their best that morning. Talk was slow coming, and there was some visible suffering. Breakfast was perfunctory and substantial. And once it was over a pickup brought a beef carcass from where it had hung since the previous weekend. Moods changed for the better. People armed themselves with knives and saws and set to work cutting the meat. Others wrapped it and marked it and carried the packages into the freezer. Hundreds of pounds of steaks, roasts, chops, ribs, chunks for stewing and hamburger were handled with amazing efficiency.

A second fire had been kindled in a large pit. When the coals were perfect, the pieces of a young goat were put on the grill and laved with barbecue sauce. The smell was sweet and sharp, and it began working on the collective appetite.

Again, there was a feast. Hangovers mostly worked away or urged into temporary submission by more beer, everyone fell to eating. The *cabrito* was succulent, Boyd's sauce a success.

After lunch, a huge dressed hog with skin the color of bread dough was brought to the cutting tables. The crew, too full of roast baby goat and beer to show much enthusiasm, sighed and went slowly back to work.

The last of the sausage was ground and packed and in the cooler by late afternoon. Then Lupe began making *chicharrónes*. These fat bits of scalded and scraped pork skin were put into a large cast-iron pan and heated over the open fire. The process rendered off the lard, which was poured boiling hot into big five-gallon containers to be used as winter shortening. The *chicharrónes* cooled to succulent golden curls.

Lupe did most of the work. It was a hot, hard job and required a practiced hand to make sure the pieces of pigskin were cooked to perfection—crisp but not overdone. Everyone else stood back and watched, reaching out now and then for a sample.

The sheriff nodded at Lupe. "I can't say as I blame them for coming over here. They're starving to death in Mexico." He went off toward his car for another beer.

A young man from Austin, who had been listening, shook his head. "God, isn't he perfect? Just the right sheriff hat, the right hair bristling up off his neck just the way it should. They must clone those bastards from some old piece of J. Edgar Hoover the government's keeping in a deep freeze somewhere."

One of the women from Alpine watched Lupe pour hot lard through a strainer into a bucket. "Animal fat!" she declared, taking a couple of *chicharrónes*. "We all need to eat more animal fat."

"Yeah, sure, you might as well stick glue in your arteries."

"Oh, you can have chelation treatment for that," she said. "Animal fat is good for you, good for the soul."

That touched off a pro-and-con discussion of fat and health, all of the participants eagerly munching on the *chicharrónes*.

Lupe finished another pot of *chicharrónes*. He stepped back from the hot mesquite fire, mopping the sweat from his face on the sleeve of his shirt. He asked if I was going to Presidio the next morning and wondered if he could catch a ride. I said he could. He explained that if he took the bus down from the other side it would take three or four hours. It was less than forty miles, but the road was so bad the bus barely crept from stop to stop.

As if the pain of the previous night had drifted completely out of memory, the drinking continued on into that night as well. There were, however, fewer takers for the sotol and far less conversation. Lupe continued to make *chicharrónes*, the light of the fire reflecting from his sweaty face. When he finally finished, exhausted and drained after so many hours of heat, he slipped away to wherever he had chosen to sleep.

The next morning he was ready, his small bag packed and set in a patch of shade on the sidewalk beside the house. We drove into Presidio, and I took him across the bridge into Ojinaga. He had talked on the way in and he continued as we sat in a bar and sipped powerful margaritas. Lupe was generous in his pronunciation of Spanish, repeating the words I didn't immediately catch. He spoke of Mexican politics, of the problems of the country, how difficult it was going to be to change Mexico without totally wiping out the present government and the mentality behind it. Among other things, he said, they had allowed the Mafia to control dope trafficking and prostitution in his home state of Chihuahua as well as in most of the other states along the border.

From the beginning I'd been amazed by this man. He'd had almost no formal education; he measured his school years by pinching his thumb and forefinger together. He had done farm and ranch work all his life, most of the time isolated from his country and his people. Nonetheless, he had an uncanny understanding of Mexico in particular and humanity in general.

In the end, spurred by the afternoon heat and the excitement of talk, we drank far too many margaritas. Lupe signaled the waiter for another round. I stopped him. I still had to drive back to Texas. Lupe insisted on paying the check. I had seen this before in Mexico. It was important to him as a man. It was the other side of machismo. The side that counted, a gesture between two new friends on the border.